T0384017

CONSUMPTION

This book provides a clear and wide-ranging overview of consumption as a sociological concept. Arguing that consumption is both an unavoidable part of life and an ongoing dialectical process, it gives a critical assessment of a range of theoretical approaches to the study of consumption and the possibilities these frameworks can offer.

Consumption is something we all do. It is not just another word for shopping. When we eat and drink, read a book or watch TV, or visit an art gallery or spend an evening in a pub, we are consuming. There is not 'a world of consumption' that some of us do not enter. We are all consumers and consumption must be regarded as an important sociological concept as a result. Consumption is also connected to notions of 'agency' – what people do, rather than what is done to them or made available to them for their doings. Before the critical focus on consumption, it was assumed that the meaning and use of things was dictated by how they were produced or by their simple mute materiality. Focusing on consumption challenges this way of thinking: rather than the mute and predictable end point of production, it is rethought as an activity, a process, something we do that involves use and meaning. It is how most of us intervene in culture.

This thought-provoking yet accessible book offers a valuable introduction of the concept of consumption for researchers and undergraduate and postgraduate students in a range of fields within the humanities and social sciences, including sociology, history, anthropology, English, media and cultural studies.

John Storey is Emeritus Professor of Cultural Studies at the Centre for Research in Media and Cultural Studies at the University of Sunderland, UK. He has published widely on cultural theory, popular culture, consumption, and utopianism. He is the author of numerous books, including *Culture and Power in Cultural Studies: The Politics of Signification* (2010), *From Popular Culture to Everyday Life* (Routledge, 2014), *Theories of Consumption* (Routledge, 2017), *Radical Utopianism and Cultural Studies: On Refusing to be Realistic* (Routledge, 2019), *Cultural Theory and Popular Culture: An Introduction* (Ninth Edition, Routledge, 2021), and *Consuming Utopia: Cultural Studies and the Politics of Reading* (Routledge, 2022). He is also the editor of *The Making of English Popular Culture* (Routledge, 2016) and *Cultural Theory and Popular Culture: A Reader* (Routledge, 2019).

KEY IDEAS
Series Editor: Anthony Elliott

Designed to complement the successful *Key Sociologists*, this series covers the main concepts, issues, debates, and controversies in sociology and the social sciences. The series aims to provide authoritative essays on central topics of social science, such as community, power, work, sexuality, inequality, benefits and ideology, class, family, etc. Books adopt a strong 'individual' line, as critical essays rather than literature surveys, offering lively and original treatments of their subject matter. The books will be useful to students and teachers of sociology, political science, economics, psychology, philosophy, and geography.

SOCIAL CAPITAL (3RD EDITION)
JOHN FIELD

PATRIARCHY
PAVLA MILLER

POPULISM: AN INTRODUCTION
MANUEL ANSELMI

COMMUNITY (3RD EDITION)
GERARD DELANTY

WELFARE CONDITIONALITY
BETH WATTS AND SUZANNE FITZPATRICK

THE STRANGER
SHAUN BEST

SECULARIZATION
CHARLES TURNER

UNIVERSAL BASIC INCOME
BRIAN MCDONOUGH AND JESSIE BUSTILLOS MORALES

REFUGIA
RADICAL SOLUTIONS TO MASS DISPLACEMENT
ROBIN COHEN AND NICHOLAS VAN HEAR

POSTCOLONIAL EUROPE
LARS JENSEN

EXCEPTIONALISM
LARS JENSEN AND KRISTÍN LOFTSDÓTTIR

CONSUMPTION
JOHN STOREY

For a full list of titles in this series, please visit www.routledge.com/Key-Ideas/book-series/SE0058

CONSUMPTION

John Storey

LONDON AND NEW YORK

Cover image: Getty Images

First published 2023
by Routledge
4 Park Square, Milton Park, Abingdon, Oxon OX14 4RN

and by Routledge
605 Third Avenue, New York, NY 10158

Routledge is an imprint of the Taylor & Francis Group, an Informa business

British Library Cataloguing-in-Publication Data
A catalogue record for this book is available from the British Library

Library of Congress Cataloging-in-Publication Data
Names: Storey, John, 1947- author.
Title: Consumption / John Storey.
Description: Abingdon, Oxon ; New York, NY : Routledge, 2023. |
Series: Key ideas | Includes bibliographical references and index. |
Identifiers: LCCN 2022022283 (print) | LCCN 2022022284 (ebook) |
ISBN 9781032124193 (hardback) | ISBN 9781032124216 (paperback) |
ISBN 9781003224471 (ebook)
Subjects: LCSH: Consumption (Economics)--Social aspects.
Classification: LCC HC79.C6 S76 2023 (print) | LCC HC79.C6 (ebook) |
DDC 339.4/7--dc23/eng/20220516
LC record available at https://lccn.loc.gov/2022022283
LC ebook record available at https://lccn.loc.gov/2022022284

ISBN: 978-1-032-12419-3 (hbk)
ISBN: 978-1-032-12421-6 (pbk)
ISBN: 978-1-003-22447-1 (ebk)

DOI: 10.4324/9781003224471

Typeset in Bembo
by KnowledgeWorks Global Ltd.

For Charlie, Jenny, Lily, and Thomas

CONTENTS

FIGURES

TABLES

CONSUMPTION AS A KEY SOCIOLOGICAL CONCEPT

In this introductory chapter, I explain how consumption is a key sociological concept for two reasons: it is something we all do, and for what it reveals about human agency. I then distinguish between consumption in general, which has been part of all human history, and specific forms of consumption that are always historically situated. Consumption, as we experience it, is a fundamental part of what we call capitalist consumerism. The chapter then discusses consumption as a process. Instead of it being understood as a single event, the moment of purchase, I argue that it consists of a series of moments. There are at least four aspects to processes of consumption: 'why' we consume, 'what' is consumed, 'how' it is consumed, and any 'effects' of what is consumed. The chapter concludes with an exploration of how different theoretical approaches construct their own understanding of consumption as an object of study. Therefore, what counts as consumption will vary from chapter to chapter.

THE ORDINARINESS OF CONSUMPTION

Consumption is something we all do. It is not just another word for shopping. When we eat and drink, read a book or watch TV, or visit an art gallery or spend an evening in a pub, we are consuming. There is not 'a world of consumption' that some of us do not enter. We are all consumers and that is the first reason why consumption is an important sociological concept: it aids analysis of our interactions with each other and the world around us (see Chapters 3 and 5).[1]

DOI: 10.4324/9781003224471-1

Consumption is also a key concept in sociological analysis for another reason: its connection to notions of 'agency' – what people do, rather than what is done to them or made available to them for their doings. Before the critical focus on consumption, it was assumed that the meaning and use of things was dictated by how they were produced or their simple mute materiality (see Chapter 3). The new concept of consumption challenges this way of thinking: rather than the mute and predictable end point of production, it is rethought as an activity, a process, something we do that involves use and meaning. It is how most of us intervene in culture (see Chapters 2, 4, and 7).

Therefore, unlike the very influential *Empire of Things* (Trentmann, 2017), this book will not treat what is offered for consumption as if this counts as consumption itself. In Frank Trentmann's account, consumption and what is offered for consumption are interchangeable. This is often consumption at one remove. It explains it as an essential feature of the development of capitalism but rarely explores actual practices of consumption or the theoretical traditions which have tried to understand such practices. We might know that reading increased or decreased in a particular social context, but this tells us nothing about what people read and why and how they read and what effects their reading might produce. Trentmann discusses the supply of water, gas, and electricity as if he is talking about the consumption of these utilities. He does something similar in terms of the growth of the film industry. But supply is not the same as consumption. How people consume is not the same as what they consume. The use and meaning of cinema cannot be determined by cataloguing what is available to view. This is more about the availability of things, than about their use and signification. There is very little about consumption as it exists as a key concept in sociological analysis. It is against this kind of approach that the rise of consumption in sociology and elsewhere was intended to challenge. In this sense, Trentmann's book is a story of structures, a narrative of consumption as something made available by capitalism. There is very little about the agency of actual practices of consumption. Although it draws heavily on research in sociology and cultural studies, paradoxically, it is a book that could have been written before these disciplines argued for the investigation of agency as it is caught in an endless dance of structure and agency.

CONSUMPTION AND CAPITALIST CONSUMERISM

While it is true that the desire for material things is not something invented by capitalism, the desire for such things has undoubtedly increased massively during the 500 years of its existence as the dominant mode of production. We should not be surprised by this, as consumption is necessary for the reproduction of a system based on never-ending increases in production. Accumulation or the search for profit is a capitalist imperative; it has an absolute need to exploit labour and appropriate nature. Put simply, capitalism cannot rely on satisfying wants; it must create them. Without increasing consumption, it would be unable to reproduce itself. Therefore, it has worked very hard to redefine us all as consumers, living in a consumer society.

While it is imperative not to confuse consumption with consumerism, it is nevertheless important to acknowledge that consumption, as discussed in this book, takes place in a particular historical context, capitalist consumer society. Karl Marx distinguishes between 'production in general' and specific historical modes of production. As he explains it, production in general 'is common to all social conditions, that is without historic character, *human*' (1973: 320). But the human need to produce is always located historically in a particular mode of production: i.e., humans have always produced but how they produce is always historically situated. In other words, there is a difference between a slave mode of production and a capitalist mode of production. If we think of this in terms of consumption, we arrive at similar conclusions: there is 'consumption in general' and there are specific modes of consumption. Humans have always consumed, but in different historical periods, we have consumed differently. As Marx points out,

> Hunger is hunger, but the hunger gratified by cooked meat eaten with a knife and fork is a different hunger from that which bolts down raw meat with the aid of hand, nail and tooth. Production thus produces not only the object but also the manner of consumption, not only objectively but also subjectively. Production thus creates the consumer. (92)

Our contemporary attitudes to consumption, our consumption practices, and our consumption desires have developed alongside the historical development of capitalism as a mode of production (see Chapter 4). Put simply, consumerism is the capitalist version of consumption; it is a particular historical mode of consumption unique to this historical mode of production. Consumerism is not, therefore, just consumption, it is increasingly a way of life, producing a sense – what Antonio Gramsci would call a 'common sense' (1971) – that who we are is defined and expressed through the commodities we consume. Consumerism is a practice that seeks to define people first and foremost as consumers. Moreover, it is a way of life that is dependent on more of the same – i.e., more capitalism.

One of the things that makes consumption under capitalism different is that the vast majority of what we consume has been produced as commodities to be sold for profit. Consumerism depends on a world of things. As Marx explains in the opening sentence of volume one of *Capital*, 'The wealth of societies in which the capitalist mode of production prevails appears as an immense collection of commodities' (1976a: 127). Commodities have three features: 'exchange-value', 'use-value', and 'value'. Exchange-value is the price a commodity can secure in the marketplace. To achieve this, it must have a use-value (i.e., be of use to someone). But underpinning these two values is what Marx calls value and this is measured by the 'human labour ... objectified or materialized in it' (129). Moreover, as he explains, 'A commodity appears at first sight an extremely obvious, trivial thing. But its analysis brings out that it is a very strange thing, abounding in metaphysical subtleties and theological niceties' (163). The strangeness of the commodity does not arise from its exchangeability or from its use-value, but from its concealment of human labour. In a capitalist economy, commodities seem to exist only in relation to one another. However, what appear to be relations between things are in fact relations between people. Commodity exchange, Marx argues,

> It is nothing but the definite social relation between men themselves which assumes here, for them, the fantastic form of a relation between things. In order, therefore, to find an analogy we must take flight into the misty realm of religion. There

the products of the human brain appear as autonomous figures endowed with a life of their own, which enter into relations both with each other and with the human race. So it is in the world of commodities with the products of men's hands. I call this the fetishism which attaches itself to the products of labour as soon as they are produced as commodities and is therefore inseparable from the production of commodities. (165)

According to Marx, the 'fetishism of the world of commodities arises from the peculiar social character of the labour which produces them' (ibid.). In previous modes of production, the social relations of work are clear and direct; it is only under capitalism that they are concealed behind the exchange of commodities. If I make something and then exchange it for something made by another person, the social relations of work are plain to see. If I am a slave and make something, which you use, again the social relations of work are very clear. But if I make something for a capitalist in return for wages, what I make and what others make now exists in the marketplace for me to purchase with money. What I make becomes a commodity available to me if I have sufficient funds to purchase it. What another worker makes is also available for me to buy if I can afford it. The products of our labour now exist as commodities that circulate as exchange-values to be converted for money into use-values. The value embodied in the commodity by labour is now concealed beneath exchange-value and use-value.

Further to this, commodity fetishism conceals from me the conditions of labour behind what I buy. If I go to a supermarket to buy oranges, I may know from which country the oranges originate, but it is unlikely I will know the social conditions of their production. My relationship to the labour of others is thus concealed in a relationship between things – my money and the fruit offered for sale. In this way, then, when we go shopping, we are surrounded by commodities seemingly supplied by the market and available for us to consume by the means of money. But behind all this, and hidden by commodity fetishism, are the conditions of human labour. What is also often hidden is exploitation on a massive scale. What is made for very little in the so-called Third World is often sold for significantly more in the First. For example, t-shirts made to promote the Walt Disney film *Pocahontas* sold for $10.97 each in the USA. The workers making the t-shirts earned $2.22 for an eight-hour day in which they would make 50 t-shirts with a total value of $548.50 (Kernaghan, 1997: 101). Although this is clearly outrageous, it is only a very profitable exaggeration of the normal practices of capitalism. As David Harvey observes, 'To pretend this all arrives magically through the market, facilitated by the magic of money that happens to be in our pocket, is to succumb totally to the fetishism of the commodity' (2010: 61).

Commodity fetishism, in other words, arises from the concealment of the social relations of human labour behind the exchange of commodities. But what ultimately defines commodities, what they all have in common, is not use-value or exchange-value (these are various and variable) but the fact that they all embody what Marx calls the 'phantom-like objectivity' (1976a: 128) of human labour. This phantom presence is concealed behind the language of exchange-value. Every time we walk around a shopping centre, we encounter commodities speaking the language of exchange-value, but behind the announcement of price and possibility is the phantom of human labour hidden from view. It would be a very different shopping experience if, say, each item of clothing we examined informed us of the human labour that produced it. Imagine looking for something new to wear, and instead of enticing images of attractive models wearing beautiful clothes, we were confronted by large photographs of children working in appalling conditions for starvation wages, accompanied by the question: *Do you now understand why this is such good value for money?*

CONSUMPTION AS PROCESS

This is primarily a book about consumption as a sociological concept. It presents a critical assessment of a range of 'theoretical approaches' to the study of consumption. In doing this, it is hoped the book will provide a clear and wide-ranging understanding of the concept as well as a good appreciation of the theoretical possibilities available when undertaking undergraduate and postgraduate work on objects of consumption. Each chapter considers consumption from a different theoretical perspective. Sometimes theory is explicit, while at other times, it is the framing discourse of a particular methodology.

However, some theories do not seem like theories at all. They appear to be simply descriptions of how the world is. What mainstream economics claims about consumption is theory masquerading as description. *Homo economicus* is the name given to the subject at the centre of much economic theory. He (rarely thought of as a she) is the consumer who makes consumption choices based on rationality and self-interest.[2] It is these choices that supposedly determine production. According to this way of thinking, all producers do is simply respond to what consumers want. Therefore, if, for example, there is a problem between human consumption and the environment, the fault lies in individual choices. Blaming the producers is simply not rational; the solution is to change consumer demand. It is an approach which assumes or at the very least has made a major contribution to the assumption that people are selfish, driven by self-interest. According to this way of thinking, regardless of how altruistic the action might appear, ultimately, we will find greed at its root.[3] In many ways, it is the guiding fairy tale of capitalist economics, supposedly explaining a whole variety of human behaviour. Wonderfully matching the reproductive needs of capitalism, it reduces consumption to the moment of purchase; everything else being considered irrelevant. But, as we shall see, any serious sociological study of consumption must consider this moment as just one in a process that involves moments before and after the moment of purchase.

Although consumption is fundamental to the very fabric of a capitalist economy, this does not mean that consumption can be reduced to a single economic event. There are at least two reasons to reject this idea. First, there are many types of consumption which do not usually involve an economic exchange – borrowing a library book, consuming a landscape, drinking water from a public fountain, receiving a gift. But there is a second reason, much more significant for thinking sociologically about the topic of this book, and that is that consumption is not a single event – a moment of acquisition – but a series of moments in a process. There are at least four aspects to processes of consumption: 'why' we consume, 'what' is consumed, 'how' it is consumed, and any 'effects' of what is consumed (see Figure 1.1). These are separate moments in a variable process. Considering which book to buy is not the same as buying a book. Buying a book is not the same as reading one.

pre-acquisition ⟶ acquisition ⟶ appropriation ⟶ effects

select book ⟶ buy book ⟶ read book ⟶ effects of reading

Figure 1.1 Consumption as process

Writing about a book or discussing it with friends is not the same as reading a book.

Economics starts and ends with purchase. But if we think of consumption as a process, we must consider these other moments. When, for example, I explore what a bookshop has to offer, this is a moment of selectivity and discrimination, an active engagement with what might be consumed. This might or might not be followed by a moment of purchase. If I buy a book and take it home to read, the act of reading is a third moment. The fourth moment is when what I have read enters something I write or conversations I have with myself or with family, friends, or colleagues. It is in the afterlife of acquisition and appropriation that people may make meaningful and entangle with memories what had once been a commodity produced for profit. Not all moments in the process will always become active with the same intensity. Appropriation, for example, will vary in different processes of consumption. It does not necessarily require that the thing in question be used up in the process of consuming. This might be the case when I buy a pizza but is certainly not when I consume a landscape or an episode of *The Handmaid's Tale*, *Succession*, or *The Leftovers*.

CONSUMPTION AS DISCOURSE

If we think of consumption as a purely economic activity, it exists only in the moment of purchase, defined by exchange-value. But once we have bought something, we do not stop consuming it. If you buy a print of a painting from a charity shop, you may look at it hundreds of times; each of these is a moment of consumption not captured by thinking of it in purely economic terms. These other moments beyond purchase are moments when consumption becomes cultural as it becomes entangled in social use and the making of meaning. As such it can be made to fulfil a wide range of social and personal purposes. What and how we consume may serve to say who we are or who we would like to be; it may be used to produce and maintain a particular lifestyle; it may promise compensation in times of loss or provide a symbolic means to celebrate success and mark achievement; it can serve to meet both our needs and our desires; it can provide the material for our dreams; it can mark and maintain social difference and social distinction, and it can be the sign of our oppression and exploitation.

In these ways, consumption becomes a changed object of study. Bente Halkier makes the valid point that, 'The international social scientific research on consumption and consumers is such a wide and interdisciplinary field that it is almost a mission impossible to construct an overview of all the different approaches to methodological design and use of methods applied within the field, which range from highly quantitative consumer behaviour analysis to deeply qualitative ethnographic consumption process studies' (2019: 36). However, while the purpose of this book is to present, in an accessible and coherent way, a critical overview of this complex and expanding field, it does not offer an *interdisciplinary* approach in which consumption, always the same, is engaged with from a range of critical perspectives. Instead of the same object of study being viewed differently, consumption changes as an object of study when caught in the critical gaze of each perspective. It is not the same object studied from a variety of perspectives; it is constructed variously depending on the discourse in which it is situated: the questions and answers will always be different. Each theoretical framing will enable and constrain a variety of forms of analysis, carrying with it a range of varying assumptions, producing distinctive problems and solutions.

To understand consumption, we must understand that it is not one thing. It exists as different things depending on in which *discourse* it is articulated. Discourse is a concept developed by the French theorist Michel Foucault. According to Foucault, discourses work in three ways: they enable, they constrain, and they constitute. As he explains, discourses are 'practices that systematically form the objects of which they speak' (1989: 49). Language, for example, is a discourse: it enables me to speak, it constrains what I can say, it constitutes me as a speaking subject (i.e., it situates and produces my subjectivity: I know myself in language; I think in language; I talk to myself in language). Academic disciplines are also discourses; like languages, they enable, constrain, and constitute.

The theoretical framing of each discipline speaks about an object of study in a particular way and in so doing it enables and constrains what can be said about it. But they do not just speak about it; by constructing it as a particular object of study, they constitute it as a specific reality ('the real meaning' of the object).

In *The History of Sexuality*, Foucault tracks the discourse of sexuality through a series of nineteenth-century discursive domains: medicine, demography, psychiatry, pedagogy, social work, criminology, government, and what we would now call sociology. Rather than silence on matters sexual (which is what we might have expected given the stereotype of Victorian prudery), he encounters instead 'a political, economic and technical incitement to talk about sex' (1981: 22–23). He argues that these different discourses on sexuality are not simply about sexuality, they constitute sexuality as an object of knowledge. This is not to say that sexuality did not exist as a non-discursive formation in nineteenth-century Europe, rather it is to recognize that our 'knowledge' of sexuality and the 'power-knowledge' relations of sexuality constituted by it are discursive. In other words, our understanding of sexuality – what we think is normal – organizes how we respond to practices of sexuality (see Storey, 2021a).

Discourse, according to Ernesto Laclau and Chantal Mouffe, consists in the totality of the linguistic and non-linguistic. They use the term discourse 'to emphasize the fact that every social configuration is meaningful. If I kick a spherical object in the street or if I kick a ball in a football match, the physical fact is the same, but its meaning is different. The object is a football only to the extent that it establishes a system of relations with other objects, and these relations are not given by the mere referential materiality of the objects, but are, rather, socially constructed. This systematic set of relations is what we call discourse' (2019: 126). Moreover,

> the discursive character of an object does not, by any means, imply putting its existence into question. The fact that a football is only a football as long as it is integrated within a system of socially constructed rules does not mean that it ceases to be a physical object .... For the same reason it is the discourse which constitutes the subject position of the social agent, and not, therefore, the social agent which is the origin of

discourse – the same system of rules that makes that spherical object into a football, makes me a player. (126–127)

In other words, objects exist independently of their discursive articulation, but it is only within discourse that they can exist as meaningful objects. For example, earthquakes exist in the real world, but whether they are

> constructed in terms of 'natural phenomena' or 'expressions of the wrath of God', depends upon the structuring of a discursive field. What is denied is not that such objects exist externally to thought, but the rather different assertion that they could constitute themselves as objects outside any discursive condition of emergence.
>
> (Laclau and Mouffe, 2001: 108)

As Gramsci points out, 'East and West ... never cease to be "objectively real" even though when analysed they turn out to be nothing more than a "historical" or "conventional construct"' (2007: 175).

> It is obvious that East and West are arbitrary and conventional (historical) constructions, since every spot on the earth is simultaneously East and West. Japan is probably the Far East not only for the European but also for the American from California and even for the Japanese himself, who, through English political culture might call Egypt the Near East .... Yet these references are real, they correspond to real facts, they allow one to travel by land and by sea and to arrive at the predetermined destination. (176)

In other words, East and West are historical constructions, directly connected to the imperial power of the West. However, they are forms of signification that have been realized and embedded in social practice: cultural constructs they may be, but they do designate real geographic locations and guide real human movement.

Concepts like consumption are not inscribed with meaning; meaning is always the result of an act of articulation. 'The practice of articulation', as Laclau and Mouffe (2001) explain, 'consists in the ... partial fix[ing] of meaning' (113). As Stuart Hall points out, 'Meaning is a social production, a practice. The world has to be made to mean' (2019: 121). The Russian theorist Valentin Volosinov argues that texts and practices, including concepts such as consumption, are 'multi-accentual': that is, they can be 'spoken' with different 'accents' by different people in different discourses and different social contexts for different purposes. That is, they can be made to mean different things in different contexts. The sign is always a potential site of 'differently oriented social interests' (1973: 23). Individual discourses tend 'to make the sign uni-accentual', to make what is potentially multi-accentual appear as if it could only ever be uni-accentual. In other words, things – including consumption – do not issue their own meanings; they provide the material for the articulation of meaning – variable meaning(s) – as things are articulated, disarticulated, and rearticulated in different contexts. So, when we encounter consumption in the remaining chapters, it may seem a different object of study as it is articulated for the purposes of a particular theoretical approach. While this does not mean that it does not exist independently of these discursive articulations, it is only within these discourses that it exists as a specific object of study. Whether it is constructed, for example, as a moment of purchase, a social practice, part of identity formation, a display of cultural capital, or an example of mediatization will depend on the structuring of a discursive field. But, to repeat, this does not mean that consumption ceases to exist outside these discourses. Rather, what is being claimed is that consumption's existence as an object of study depends on these discursive conditions of emergence. Therefore, what counts as consumption will vary from chapter to chapter, as the different theoretical approaches construct in discourse their own understanding of consumption as an object of study.

NOTES

1 Historically, consumption has two general meanings. Both derive from the word consume, which entered English from French in the fourteenth century. Consume began by meaning 'to destroy, to use up, to waste, to exhaust' (Williams 1983: 78). It is from this way of using the word that pulmonary phthisis is described as consumption. From the middle of the

eighteenth century, consumer emerges in political economy. It is also in this period that producer and consumer, production and consumption, become prominent terms in the same discourse. From around the 1950s, consumer replaces customer 'to describe a buyer or purchaser' (79). The term consumer society carries with it some of the original meanings of consume, especially waste and exhaust.

2 But, as Ian Hudson and Mark Hudson point out, 'Like the Yeti, Homo economicus is very difficult to find' (2021: 29). This is because it is an economic construct, a mythical being invented to defend the relations of consumption and production under capitalism, especially in terms of consumer sovereignty and ever-increasing market choice. It is a fundamental part of an argument for economic growth, in which more choice equals greater happiness.

3 As *The Guardian* reported in March 2021, commenting on the National Health Service's successful roll-out of the vaccine against Covid-19, Prime Minister Boris Johnson told Conservative MPs, 'The reason we have the vaccine success is because of capitalism, because of greed my friends' (https://www.theguardian.com/politics/2021/mar/23/greed-and-capitalism-behind-jab-success-boris-johnson-tells-mps).

2

WHAT DRIVES CONSUMPTION?

In this chapter, we consider four answers to the question of what drives consumption: Karl Marx's theory of alienation, historian Neil McKendrick's claims about the role of social emulation in the historical development of mass consumption, sociologist Colin Campbell's theory of the Romantic ethic, and the relationship between consumption and identity, drawing mostly on the work of cultural theorist Judith Butler.

MARX, ALIENATION, AND CONSUMPTION

According to Marx, alienation helps produce consumption.[1] Alienation occurs when we are prevented from realizing our full human capacities in acts of labour. Unable to do this, we turn to consumption in search of creative fulfilment and control. To fully comprehend this argument, we must understand Marx's view of human nature. Marx distinguishes between 'human nature in general' and 'human nature as modified in each historical epoch' (1976a: 759). Human nature in general consists of certain needs and capacities. These can be divided into those that are 'natural' and those that belong to our 'species being' (what marks us out as human). Our 'natural' needs and capacities we share with other animals (food, shelter, reproduction, etc.), while those of our 'species being' are unique to us as humans and are historically and socially variable in their concrete manifestation. In other words, and contrary to many conservative accounts, human nature is not fixed and unchanging; it is not something set, but always in a state of becoming. What it means to be human in the contemporary

DOI: 10.4324/9781003224471-2

world, with all its geographic variety, is very different from what it was 5,000 or 10,000 years ago. It will be different again in the future. We may be a biological bundle of needs and capacities, but these needs and capacities change as we change the world around us. As Marx claims, 'all history is nothing but a continual transformation of human nature' (Marx; quoted in Ollman, 1976: 79). Our humanity, like the world in which we live, is a social production.

Our species being manifests itself in two ways: subjectively in terms of our awareness of belonging to a species (we think about what it is to be human) and in the objectively realized forms such as institutions and works of art. It displays itself in our consciousness of ourselves and others acting in the world in the present, with an awareness of a past and the expectation of a future. Moreover, as humans, we not only produce, but we also consciously consider and reflect on and modify how and what we produce. Humans are said to be the only animals that act in this way.

> The animal is immediately identifiable with his life-activity. It does not distinguish itself from it. It is its life-activity. Man makes his life-activity the object of his will and of his consciousness … Conscious life-activity directly distinguishes man from animal life-activity.
>
> (Marx, 2011: 54)

In other words, we can reflect on what we are doing, both at the time of doing it and later after it has been done, whereas animals, Marx believed, just do it – they produce to satisfy immediate physical needs. We are purposive in a way that animals are not. According to Marx,

> A spider conducts operations that resemble those of a weaver, and a bee puts to shame many an architect in the construction of her cells. But what distinguishes the worst architect from the best of bees is this, that the architect raises his structure in the imagination before he erects it in reality. At the end of every labour-process, we get a result that already existed in the imagination of the labourer at its commencement. He not only effects a change of form in the material on which he works, but he also

realizes a purpose of his own that gives the law to his modus operandi, and to which he must subordinate his will.

(1976a: 284)

In this way, then, what makes us human and divides us from other animals is our capacity for reflective productive activity that goes well beyond our immediate needs. As Marx explains, making very clear the absolute importance of an expanded notion of production to include consumption, 'the productive life is the life of the species' (2011: 54). Human becoming is the gradual transformation of the natural into the human. We have biological needs and capacities, but these are worked on and as they are worked on, they become human and social. Our relationship with nature (both our own and that external to us) is socially and historically mediated. We do not just satisfy our needs or exercise our capacities, we wonder about them, we reflect on what might be best or what might be possible. We write novels and poetry about our needs and capacities; we sing songs about them; we produce films and television dramas and documentaries; we paint great works of art in an attempt to explain or celebrate them. We do not just have sex to reproduce, we do it for pleasure and for love, and we laugh and cry and dream about this in ways that are unimaginable to other animals. So, what begins as the satisfaction of a natural need or the exercise of a natural capacity is gradually transformed into a social activity that helps define us as human. What was once a simple act of nature becomes a social practice available to be mediated in the highest forms of human reflection. What was once a natural act becomes a social act entangled in history and politics, open to law and regulation, helping to define what it is to be human. But we never lose contact with nature. To paraphrase Henri Lefebvre, we separate from nature without detaching ourselves from it (2002: 192). Consumption is inseparable from these various transformations.

Marx starts his analysis of alienation from the assumption that creative labour is an essential part of our species being. Through productive activity, we externalize ourselves in the world. For example, as I write these words, I produce myself as a writer. Without writing, I cannot claim to be a writer: the words I write produce and reproduce me as a writer. According to Marx, under capitalism (although he is writing about nineteenth-century capitalism and thinking particularly of the new factory system, what he says is still relevant today), the alienation of labour manifests itself in several ways. First, the product of labour does not belong to the worker. The worker is paid to work; therefore, the person or persons who pay the wage own what the worker produces. Consequently, the worker encounters what she has produced 'as an alien object' (Marx, 2011: 53), with an existence independent of their will. That is, once her labour is 'congealed' (50) in the object produced, it takes on an existence outside of her productive activity. As Marx explains, 'The alienation of the worker in his product means not only that his labor becomes an object, an external existence, but that it exists outside him, independently, as something alien to him, and that it becomes a power on its own confronting him' (51). It is as a power confronting the worker that the second aspect of alienation becomes manifest. If I were a contemporary of Marx, a worker who baked bread, my reward would be a weekly wage. Once this wage is spent, no matter how hungry I might be, the bread I had made, the object of my labour, my labour-made material (i.e., 'congealed' in the object of my labour) would confront me in a shop as an alien object that had the power to satisfy my hunger, but which I cannot eat unless I have enough money to buy. What I have made now exists independently of my will, and I have no control over what becomes of what I have made; it is now a commodity that circulates in search of profit. To give another example, closer to home, the books I write exist in the marketplace beyond my control. If I want a new copy of one of my books, I need to have sufficient money to buy one. I cannot simply go into a shop and announce the fact that I am the author and take one from the shelf as my own: although I wrote these books, they now exist as alien objects that confront me as existing outside my productive activity.

For Marx, as has been discussed already, what defines us as humans is our productive activity, therefore, if this productive activity is realized in an object existing outside our control, an alien object, we are in some way humanly diminished. He uses the example of religion to explain his point. 'It is the same in religion. The more man puts into God, the less he retains in himself. The worker puts his life into the object; but now his life no longer belongs to him but to the object' (ibid.). We invented gods, invested them with our fears and desires, and then we let them rule over us as alien beings, independent of our will. Alienation in part happens when we take what is socially constructed or humanly made as if it were an expression of nature or divine law – the commodities the worker produces enter the marketplace as if they were objects that existed independently of her labour. As Marx further explains it,

> Just as in religion the spontaneous activity of the human imagination, of the human brain and the human heart, operates independently of the individual – that is, operates on him as an alien, divine or diabolical activity – in the same way the worker's activity is not his spontaneous activity. It belongs to another, it is the loss of his self. (52–53)

A third aspect of alienation concerns the relationship between the worker under the capitalist mode of production and her species being (as already discussed, the socially developed needs and capacities that divide us from other animals). 'In tearing away from man the object of his production ... estranged labor tears from him his species life, his real species objectivity, and transforms his advantage over animals into the disadvantage that his inorganic body, nature, is taken from him' (55). In other words, under capitalism, the worker is alienated from her 'essential nature' (ibid.). As Marx elaborates,

> the fact that labour is external to the worker, i.e., it does not belong to his essential being; that in his work, therefore, he does not affirm himself but denies himself, does not feel content but unhappy, does not develop freely his physical and mental energy but mortifies his body and ruins his mind. The worker therefore only feels himself outside his work, and in his work feels outside himself. He is at home when he is not working, and when he is working he is not at home. His labor is therefore not ... the satisfaction of a need; it is merely a means to satisfy needs external to it. (52)

If, as Marx claims, 'The object of labor is ... the objectification of man's species life' (55), the alienation of these objects to the ownership and control of another will fundamentally diminish our species being and severely stunt the realization of our full human potential. While it has always been true that we have had to work to live, under capitalism, we live to work; productive activity, the very essence of our species being, has been reduced to no other purpose than a means to stay alive and make profit for another. Put simply, most humans are redefined as workers who must consume; they are valued to the extent they produce and consume. Such a redefinition is an alienation of full 'human identity' (16).

But because of our very nature, we continue to search for our human identity. Denied to us in production, we seek it in consumption. As Marx explains, the worker 'does not fulfil himself in his work ... does not develop freely a physical and mental energy but is physically exhausted and mentally debased' (1963: 177). This situation is compounded by the fact that work 'is not the satisfaction of a need, but only a *means* for satisfying other needs' (177; original emphasis). Lacking the ability to find herself in her work (i.e., express her human creativity and control), she is forced to seek it outside her work in consumption. 'The worker therefore feels himself at home only during his leisure, whereas at work he feels homeless' (177). In other words, in search of the human identity denied in work, the worker searches for it in patterns of consumption.

SOCIAL EMULATION

Neil McKendrick identifies the practice of social emulation as a key factor in the dramatic growth of consumption in the eighteenth century:

> In imitation of the rich the middle ranks of society spent more frenziedly than ever before, and in imitation of them the rest of society joined in as best they might - and that best was unprecedented in the importance of its impact on aggregate demand. Spurred on by social emulation and class competition, men and women surrendered eagerly to the pursuit of novelty, the hypnotic effects of fashion, and the enticements of persuasive commercial propaganda.
>
> (1982: 11)

The practice of social emulation, he argues, was facilitated by three factors. First, the proximity of the different social classes played a key role, in that it provided possibilities for social mobility, social competition, and, of course, social emulation. The second factor was what he calls 'the compulsive power of fashion begotten by social competition' (ibid.). He argues that the size and nature of London was the third important factor. As he points out, the population of London increased from 200,000 in 1600 to 900,000 in 1800, making it the largest city in Europe. In addition to this, by 1750, 11 per cent of the population of England lived in the city, making London the European city with the highest proportion of total population living in its confines. When the number of visitors to London is added to the indigenous population (he estimates that up to 16 per cent of the adult population of late eighteenth-century England would have spent some time in London), and then one thinks of how all these people may have been 'exposed to the influence of London's shops, London's lifestyle and the prevailing London fashions, its potential for influencing consumer behaviour was enormous' (21). In this way, he contends, London 'served as a shopwindow for the whole country, the centre of forms of conspicuous consumption which would be eagerly mimicked elsewhere' (ibid.). The poet Robert Southey, writing in 1807, had no doubts about the commercial appeal of the capital:

> If I were to pass the remainder of my life in London I think the shops would always continue to amuse me. Something extraordinary or beautiful is for ever to be seen in them … There is a perpetual exhibition of whatever is curious in nature or art, exquisite in workmanship, or singular in costume; and the display is perpetually varying as the ingenuity of trade and the absurdity of fashion are ever producing something new.
>
> (quoted in McKendrick, 1982: 78)

McKendrick argues that social emulation and 'the manipulation of social emulation [through advertising and sales campaigns] made men [and women] pursue "luxuries" where they had previously bought "decencies", and "decencies" where they had previously bought only "necessities"' (98). Social emulation and the manipulation of social emulation were driven by the emergence in the eighteenth century of what he calls the 'Western European fashion pattern' (41), characterized by the rapid speed of change. He points to the key role played by manipulation:

> potent as the force of fashion was, it needed to be released and mobilized and exploited before it could significantly add to aggregate demand. The conditions making this possible grew steadily more favourable ... But it still required active and aggressive selling to reach that market and exploit its full potential. (63)

If social emulation is to have an impact on production, it requires to be matched by emulative spending. McKendrick argues that domestic servants played a crucial role in the transmission of consumer taste and behaviour from the dominant classes in the metropolis to other classes in the provinces. In this way, he maintains, social emulation flowed downwards from the rich to their domestic servants, then to industrial workers, and finally to agricultural workers. Working in this way, he argues, social emulation 'became an engine for growth, a motive power for mass production' (1982: 66). But as Ben Fine and Ellen Leopold point out, 'Emulative spending developing from below stairs appears highly improbable' (1990: 169). They cite the example of Barbara Johnson, who in the 1760s paid £7 15s 9d for material to make a day dress, at a time when her housemaid's basic annual salary would have been about £7 7s. It therefore seems highly unlikely that domestic servants engaged in emulative spending. The clothes they wore that echoed their employers' tastes were handed down from mistress to maid. Fine and Leopold offer two reasons for this. The first is the increasing pace of fashion among the dominant classes in late eighteenth-century England. The other reason presents a direct challenge to the very idea of social emulation: 'Employers often selected and purchased clothes for their servants to wear ... [because servants'] clothes were a highly visible sign of their employers' wealth and status ... [they] reflected his or her taste, not that of the servant' (170).

Historian Ann Bermingham is also critical of the use of social emulation as a model for understanding the growth of mass consumption. She thinks it an inadequate approach to the processes and patterns of consumption in that it always assumes a top-down flow of cultural influence. As a model of explanation, she claims, it always 'reinforces the political view that culture is the province of the elite' (1995: 12).[2] Moreover, such arguments, she observes, always draw their evidence from the self-understanding and self-presentation of dominant voices in past periods in history. Such unproblematic use of the views expressed by dominant voices may lead to a failure by historians to penetrate beneath the surface discourse to reveal what might be the ideological stake that these voices have in specific arguments about social emulation. For example, as Bermingham makes clear, expressions of distaste at people supposedly consuming above their station might be driven by a fear that such an activity might lead to other, more socially threatening, ideas and practices. In other words, the reality might be that the dominant voices are really articulating their fear of where social emulation might lead, rather than identifying actual instances of it in practice. In addition to this, Bermingham further observes, '[t]he top-down model of emulation is also flawed in that it cannot accommodate situations where cultural forms seem to flow in the reverse direction' (ibid.). Fine and Leopold, for instance, cite the eighteenth-century example of social emulation working upwards: the frock-coat's movement from being the work wear of agricultural labourers to becoming the fashion wear of members of the royal family (1990: 172).

The feminist historian Amanda Vickery is also of the view that social emulation offers an inadequate explanation for the growth in mass consumption in the late eighteenth century. She argues that as a model of explanation, it presents an 'unimaginative interpretation of human motivation' in its assumption that 'envy and wishful thinking are the norm' (1993: 275). Furthermore, she contends that it is a model, especially as used by McKendrick, that often operates with a very particular view of women, as on the one hand driven by a 'pathological desire to consume', and on the other 'simply innately covetous and congenitally wistful about the prospect of upward mobility' (277). For example, whereas Harold Perkin makes a general claim about the causes of the supposed consumer revolution – 'the key to that demand was social emulation, keeping up with the Joneses, the compulsive urge for imitating the spending habits of one's betters' (1968: 110),

McKendrick is quite explicit about the gender of those doing the consuming:

> Her increased earnings released her desire to compete with social superiors, a desire pent up for centuries or at least restricted to very occasional excess.... It was this new consumer demand, the mill girl who wanted to dress like a duchess ... which helped to create the industrial revolution.
>
> (1974: 200, 209)

Vickery argues that much of this way of situating women in the practices of consumption derives from an uncritical reading of historical sources. As she explains, 'Generalizations about this homogeneously feminine consumer motivation are illustrated by uncritical quotation from eighteenth-century travellers' reports, satirical social commentary and moralists' diatribes.... Ancient prejudices have thus been passed off as actual behaviour' (277). Vickery also points out how the social emulation model has a tendency to foreshorten and impoverish analysis of consumption by 'assuming that beyond their material function goods only convey information about competitive status and sexuality and that consumables once possessed carry the same social and personal meanings for all consumers' (ibid.). Against such a position, she argues for a view of consumption 'as a positive contribution to the creation of culture and meaning' (278). In her own research, she seeks to 'move beyond the moment of purchase', to the way goods are 'used and the multitude of meanings invested in possessions over time' as they are placed in new contexts and in new relationships with other goods (281, 282). It is important, she maintains, if we are to fully understand consumption, that we try to track items as they enter the personal economy of the consumer, where they may be given new meanings, as they are placed in shifting contexts and changing relationships; they become part of the processes she calls 'inconspicuous consumption' (284). As an example of these processes, she cites research she carried out on Ellen Weeton Stock, a woman who worked as a governess in early nineteenth-century Lancashire. In a letter to her daughter Mary, written to accompany several family heirlooms, Stock wrote,

The green ribbon is part of a boxful my mother once had; they were taken in a prize which my father captured during the American war.... The piece of patchwork is an old quilt, I made it about 20 years ago; the hexagon in the middle was of our best bed hangings ... they were chintzes my father brought home with him from one of his voyages.... I am thus minded, my Mary, that you might know something of the history of your mother's family.

(quoted in Vickery, 1993: 293–294)

Each item is valued for its meaning rather than its material substance or monetary value.

One final problem with the social emulation model is, as sociologist Colin Campbell observes, 'behaviour which is imitative is not necessarily also emulative' (1993: 40). That is to say, a domestic servant may wear a dress similar to one worn by her aristocratic employer without this necessarily implying that she is seeking to be like her mistress. Although it is the case that domestic servants accepted new and second-hand clothes from their employers, the significance and meaning of such acceptance may not be entirely self-evident. As Vickery suggests,

it is not clear that wearing a lady's dress made a parlour maid look, feel or get treated like a lady. To presume she wished she was a lady might seem legitimate, but certainly does not follow from evidence that she accepted a second-hand dress. After all, second-hand dresses could be attractive simply because they had a high resale value. Besides, the strenuous efforts ex-servants made to retrieve their wages and wardrobe, including the threat of legal action, suggest that clothing was seen as an important part of their earnings, rather than merely the coveted equipment of social emulation.

(1993: 284)

THE ROMANTIC ETHIC

Campbell argues that to fully understand the development of modern forms of consumption, we need to consider what he calls the Romantic ethic. In what he describes as 'a very ambitious argument' (1987: 2), he maintains that Romanticism, the intellectual and artistic movement which developed alongside the industrial revolution, played a crucial role in the development and rapid growth of consumer society in the late eighteenth century.

Campbell begins his argument with a process the German sociologist Max Weber (1965) referred to as 'disenchantment'. Weber used the term to describe a historical process in which emotions are gradually removed from the natural world ('the night was frightening') to be relocated in the inner world of the individual ('she experienced the night as frightening'). This is an important part of the historical development of a growing separation of the subjective inner world of the self and the objective outer world of nature. It gradually produces a way of being in the world in which there is the objective world outside the self and the subjective response to it. As Campbell comments,

> Objective reality and subjective response were now mediated through consciousness in such a way that the individual had a wide degree of choice concerning exactly how to connect them. Beliefs, actions, aesthetic preferences and emotional responses were no longer automatically dictated by circumstances but 'willed' by individuals.
>
> (1987: 73–74)

According to Campbell, this process reached a crucial stage with the development of Romanticism and what the Romantic poet Samuel Taylor Coleridge called for the first time 'self-consciousness' (73).

The importance of Romanticism for Campbell is that it was the first cultural movement committed to 'a radically different doctrine of the person' (1983: 286).

> Romanticism ... led to the creation of a distinctive ideal of character, one which, although most obviously applied to the artist, was also meant to serve for the consumer or 're-creator' of his [or her] products. Since the key characteristic of the divine was taken to be creativity, both in the sense of productivity and of originality, imagination became the most significant and prized of personal qualities, with the capacity to manifest this both in

works of art and through an ability to enter fully into those created by others acting as unambiguous signs of its presence. (52)

The Romantic concept of the self involved the view that one should
trust one's feelings; that one should seek within for guidance. This
led to what we might call a commitment to experience; that is,
a doctrine which maintains that one should seek out experiences
and then learn from these experiences; and if one is an artist, one
should express one's experiences so that others may in turn learn
from the expression of experience. The Romantics believed firmly
in the view 'that happiness comes from "self-expression"' (285).
Campbell argues that 'the romantic doctrine of learning through
experiencing tended to emphasise the value not just of all feelings
(whether positive or negative) but especially that of pleasure ....
[what William Wordsworth called] "the grand elementary principle of pleasure"' (286). This commitment to experiencing pleasure,
Campbell argues, 'is a doctrine which provides an intellectual jus-
tification to the consumptive mode as via powerful experience we
can come to know the world and ourselves' (287). It is this new
way of thinking and being in the world, the Romantic self, with its
redefinition of the individual and how to improve the individual
through exposure to many new and different experiences, which
Campbell sees as crucial to the development of a consumption
ethic. To establish an informing connection between Romanticism
and this new consumption ethic, Campbell argues that the best
place to look is in its 'development of new doctrines of art and the
artist, doctrines which of necessity also applied to the consumer of
these products' (288).[3]

Romanticism advocated an expressive theory of art; the work of
art was seen as an expression of the artist's 'genius'; an embodiment
of her experience, imagination, and feeling (see Abrams, 1953). But
crucially for the development of a consumption ethic, Romanticism
did not just advocate a new view of the production of art, but it also
insisted that the consumption of art should be understood differently. The value of consuming Romantic art was in that it gave the
consumer access to the artist's genius. Consuming Romantic art,
in other words, involved the re-creation of the artist's experience,
imagination, and feeling. As Romantic poet Percy Bysshe Shelley
argued in *A Defence of Poetry* (first published in 1821),

A man, to be greatly good, must imagine intensely and comprehensively; he must put himself in the place of another and of many others; the pains and pleasures of his species must become his own. The great instrument of moral good is the imagination; and poetry administers to the effect by acting upon the cause. Poetry enlarges the circumference of the imagination by replenishing it with thoughts of ever new delight .... Poetry strengthens that faculty which is the organ of the moral nature of man, in the same manner as exercise strengthens a limb.

(2009: 682)

The Romantic theory of poetry demands of readers an active and imaginative engagement with poetry, one, that is, which is capable of re-creating (in the act of reading) the written manifestation of the experience, the feelings, and the imagination of the poet. As Campbell explains,

It is noticeable how such a theory [the Romantic theory of poetry] places almost as much emphasis upon the 're-creative' abilities of the reader as upon the original creative faculties of the poet, for whilst the latter must be moved by what he sees, and also capable of translating this experience into an affective, and hence effective, work of art, the former must possess sufficient imaginative skill to be able to use the words on the page to produce a convincing illusion. The reader is also, in that sense, assumed to be a creative artist, capable of conjuring up images which have the power to 'move' him.

(1987: 189)

Campbell argues that the Romantic theory of poetry, with its belief in moral renewal through pleasure, 'led to the creation of a distinctive ideal of character, one which, although most obviously applied to the artist, was also meant to serve for the consumer or "re- creator" of his [or her] products' (193).

Romanticism provided that philosophy of 'recreation' necessary for a dynamic consumerism: a philosophy which legitimates the search for pleasure as a good in itself ... [In this way it,] served to provide ethical support for that restless and continuous pattern of consumption which so distinguishes the behaviour of modern man [sic]. (201)

Campbell argues, 'romantic doctrines provided a new set of motivations and justifications for consuming cultural products, ones which emphasized the value of the subjectively-apprehended experience of consumption itself' (1983: 289).[4]

Having established the origins of the dominant mode of modern consumption in both the theoretical concerns and practical consequences of Romanticism, Campbell then elaborates a more detailed theory of contemporary consumption. He begins by distinguishing between two forms of hedonism, traditional and modern. What marks the difference between these two modes is an expansion of the field of pleasure from a location in quite specific experiences to a belief that it can be in all experiences. The movement from one to the other is the result of a shift from seeking pleasure in 'sensations' to seeking pleasure in 'emotions'. As he explains,

> The key to the development of modern hedonism lies in the shift of primary concern from sensations to emotions, for it is only through the medium of the latter that powerful and prolonged stimulation can be combined with any significant degree of autonomous control, something which arises directly from the fact that an emotion links mental images with physical stimuli.
>
> (1987: 69)

In other words, traditional hedonism sought pleasure in particular objects and practices, whereas modern hedonism seeks pleasure in the meaning of objects and practices (76). Table 2.1 presents Peter Corrigan's useful diagrammatic summary of Campbell's argument.

According to Campbell, the shift from seeking pleasure in what is known to provide pleasure to seeking it in what has yet to be experienced as pleasurable had a dramatic effect on consumption. As he explains,

> The capacity to gain pleasure from self-constructed, imaginative experience crucially alters the essential nature of all

Table 2.1 Traditional versus modern hedonism

Traditional hedonism	Modern hedonism
Search for pleasure tied to specific practices	Search for pleasure in any or all experiences
Pleasure tied to sensations	Pleasure tied to emotions
Emotions not under control of subject	Emotions controlled by subject
Pleasure derived from control of objects and events	Pleasure derived from control of the meanings of objects and events

Source: Corrigan (1997: 16).

hedonistic activity.... In the ... traditional pattern of hedonistic conduct imagination does not have a significant role to play because the nature of anticipated pleasure is known from past experience. The expectation of pleasure triggers desire but what one 'expects' to enjoy is mainly what one 'remembers' enjoying. Novel objects or activities thus tend to be regarded with suspicion as their potential for pleasure is as yet unknown. In modern hedonism, on the other hand, if a product is capable of being represented as possessing unknown characteristics then it is open to the pleasure-seeker to imagine the nature of its gratifications and it thus becomes an occasion for day-dreaming. Although employing material from memory, the hedonist can now imaginatively speculate upon what gratifications and enjoyments are in store, and thus attach his [or her] favoured day-dream to this real object of desire. In this way, imagined pleasures are added to those already encountered and greater desire is experienced for the unknown than the known. (85–86)

Campbell sees this as the key to modern patterns of consumption:

The introduction of day-dreaming into hedonism thus not only strengthens desire, but helps to make desiring itself a pleasurable activity. Whilst for traditional man deferred gratification had simply meant the experience of frustration, for modern man it becomes a happy hiatus between desire and consummation which can be filled with the joys of day-dreaming. This reveals a unique feature of modern self-illusory hedonism – the fact that the desiring mode constitutes a state of enjoyable discomfort, and that wanting rather than having is the main focus of pleasure-seeking. (86)

For Campbell, the process is driven forward by the inevitable gap which always opens between the attainment of an object of desire in actuality and the anticipation of its attainment in imagination. It is generally the case that the actual experience of consumption will fail to match the experience imagined in anticipation. In this way, 'The consummation of desire is thus a necessarily disillusioning experience', in that the gap between anticipation and reality will always produce, regardless of the pleasures actual experience of consumption may bring, a 'resultant recognition that something is missing' (ibid.). Although Campbell's argument is that consumers are driven from object to object, from anticipatory day-dreaming to disillusioning reality, longing for an object of desire which can be experienced in actuality as it is experienced in imaginative anticipation, his 'central insight [however] ... is the realization that individuals do not so much seek satisfaction from products, as pleasures from self-illusory experiences which they construct from their associated meanings' (89). In this way, he argues,

The essential activity of consumption is thus not the actual selection, purchase or use of products, but the imaginative pleasure-seeking to which the product image lends itself, 'real' consumption being largely a resultant of this 'mentalistic' hedonism. Viewed in this way, the emphasis upon novelty as well as that upon insatiability both become comprehensible.

(ibid.)

It is the cycle of anticipation and disillusionment which drives the desire to consume. All that is required to keep the process moving is the appearance of new commodities for consumption. Campbell's argument is a refutation of claims that modern consumerism is evidence of a greedy materialistic desire to consume more and more objects.

The idea that contemporary consumers have an insatiable desire to acquire objects represents a serious misunderstanding of the mechanism which impels people to want goods. Their basic motivation is the desire to experience in reality the pleasurable dramas which they have already enjoyed in imagination, and each 'new' product is seen as offering a possibility of realizing this ambition. However, since reality can never provide the perfected pleasures encountered in day-dreams (or, if at all, only in part, and very occasionally), each purchase leads to literal disillusionment, something which explains how wanting is extinguished so quickly, and why people dis-acquire goods as rapidly as they acquire them. What is not extinguished, however, is the fundamental longing which day-dreaming itself generates, and hence there is as much determination as ever to find new products to serve as replacement objects of desire. (89–90)

It is the continual dynamic interaction between anticipated experience and actual experience, and the profound longing to close the gap between the two, which is the key to understanding the limitless nature of modern consumption (see Figure 2.1).

Although Campbell acknowledges the ways in which advertisers may attempt to fuel this process, he rejects the view that they can in any way control the cycle of production and reproduction of longing. He recognizes that 'advertisers [may] make use of the fact that people day-dream, and indeed feed those dreams' (91). But, as he insists, because 'the practice of day-dreaming is itself endemic to modern societies [it] does not require the commercial institution of advertising to ensure its continued existence' (ibid.).

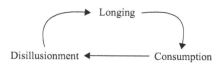

Figure 2.1 Cycle of consumption
Source: Campbell (1987).

To work as material for day-dreams, commodities must be actively consumed. Moreover, in an important distinction, running counter to much 'common sense' about consumption, Campbell is insistent that it is important 'to conceive of these … products as providing the material for day-dreams rather than as being day-dreams' (93). The activity of the consumer is crucial.

> [It] is important not only because the individual has to actively use the words, pictures, and sounds to construct an 'as-if' world for himself [sic] to inhabit, but also because the process of day-dreaming (which has in any case preceded contact with the … item in question) may well continue long after direct contact has ceased; images relating to a particular film or novel being brought to mind subsequently and embroidered in pleasurable fashion.
>
> (ibid.)

However, although consumption is an active process, the essential activity of the consumer is in the imaginative process of seeking pleasure. This leads to a concern 'with the "meaningfulness" of products', rather than 'a concern with the meaning of a product' (1995: 120).[5]

CONSUMPTION AND PERFORMATIVITY

Material things are important to us, not just for what they do or enable us to do, but for what they signify to us and to others about us. What we consume is important to our sense of who we are and who we would like others to recognize us to be. The sense that consumption and identity are inseparably entangled is not a new idea. In 1890, the philosopher William James, with a very specific class and gender focus, argued that 'A man's Self is the sum total of all that he can call his, not only his body and his psychic powers, but his clothes and his house, his wife and his children, his ancestors and friends, his reputation and works, his lands, and yacht, and bank-account' (quoted in Trentmann, 2017: 233). While most people reading this book might construct a very different list, they would probably share with James the idea of a critical connection between consumption and identity.

We all engaged in identity tourism as we change our patterns of consumption to articulate different aspects of who we are, or what we want to be. Identity is always a work in progress; a becoming rather than a fixed state of being. When we meet someone for the first time, to get to know the kind of person they are, we ask certain questions. An obvious question is what kind of work they do. But sooner or later, to get to know them better, we will ask questions about matters of consumption. What books do they read? What films do they watch? Do they have favourite television programmes? To what kinds of music do they listen? Which football team do they support? Where do they go on holiday? These questions, and many more like them, all connect consumption with identity. On knowing the answer to enough of these questions, we feel able to locate the person in a particular cultural and social space; we begin, in other words, to think we know who they are.

Traditionally, identity has usually been understood as something coherent and fixed, an essential quality of a person that is guaranteed by human nature. Against this, more recent accounts posit identity, not as something fixed and coherent, but as something constructed and always in a process of change. This is identity as 'production' rather than inheritance. It is identity constituted in, not outside, history and culture. Moreover, according to this model, the concept of identity is itself replaced by the concept of identities; that is, multiple and mobile identities. For example, Stuart Hall argues that identities are a form of consumption or secondary production (see Chapter 3). As he explains, 'identities are about questions of using the resources of history, language and culture in the process of becoming rather than being' (1996a: 4). Although identities are clearly about 'who we think we are' and 'where we think we came from', they are also about 'where we are going'. They are always a narrative of the self *becoming*. If you ask who I am, I will tell you a story. In this sense, as Hall points out, identities are increasingly less about 'roots' and more about 'routes' (ibid.). They are positions we occupy and vacate, in a never-ending journey of self-formation. So, for example, I may be at one moment a supporter of Manchester United, at another a university professor, at another a father, and at another a friend. Each of these moments has an appropriate context of articulation and specific patterns of consumption. That is, depending on context, our identities form hierarchies of the self. In specific contexts, the identity 'in dominance' may be one thing; in another context, it might be something quite different. But these other non-dominant identities are always present, always waiting ready to play a part in the changing formation of the self. Therefore, in a situation where being a Manchester United supporter is my most important identity, how I might perform this identity may well be limited by the fact that I am still a university professor. Moreover, each of these identities is entangled with consumption. Or to put it another way, what we consume and how we consume it says a great deal about who we are, who we want to be, and how others see us. Consumption is perhaps one of the most significant ways we perform our sense of self. What we consume provides us with materials with which we can stage and perform in a variety of ways the drama of who we are and how we want to be seen.

One of the most influential ways of thinking about identity in relationship to consumption can be found in Judith Butler's work on sex, gender, and performativity. Butler begins from Simone de Beauvoir's observation that 'one is not born a woman, but, rather, becomes one' (de Beauvoir, 1984: 12). Although de Beauvoir's argument has the advantage of seeing gender as something made in culture and not something fixed by nature, the problem with this model of sex and gender, according to Butler, is that it assumes that male and female biology is outside culture. Against this, she argues that biology is itself always already culturally gendered as 'male' and 'female' and, as such, already guarantees versions of the feminine and the masculine. In other words, the distinction between sex and gender is not a distinction between nature and culture; it is between two versions of the cultural. Therefore, as she contends 'one is not born a woman, one becomes one; but further, one is not born female, one becomes female' (1999: 33).

Butler's argument is that gender is not the expression of biological sex, it is performatively constructed in culture and, moreover, what is constructed in culture also constructs biology as male or female. So, whereas de Beauvoir maintains that biological identity sets the limits of gender identity, Butler argues that gender identity produces biological identity. To fully comprehend this, and to appreciate its implications for an understanding of consumption and identity formation, we need to understand performativity. Butler's concept of performativity should not be confused with the idea of performance understood as a form of play-acting in which a more fundamental identity (a 'natural self') remains intact behind the theatricality of the identity on display. As she explains it, 'there is no identity behind the expressions of gender; that identity is performatively constituted by the very "expressions" that are said to be its results' (ibid.). A significant part of these expressions involves consumption. For Butler, then, what seems like the expression of biology is in fact what produces the apparent authority of the biological. In other words, the more I behave like a 'man', the more this seems to confirm the determining role of my 'male' biology. Again, to behave like a man involves specific patterns of consumption.

Butler's theory of performativity is a development of JL Austin's theory of performative language ('speech acts'). Austin divides language into two types: constative and performative. Constative language is descriptive language. The sky is blue is an example of a constative statement. Performative language, on the other hand, does not merely describe what already exists; it brings something into being. 'I now pronounce you husband and wife' is an obvious example; it does not describe something, it brings it into existence; that is, when the words are spoken by an appropriate person, they transform two single people into a married couple. As Austin explains, 'the issuing of the utterance is the performing of an action' (1962: 6). Butler argues that gender works in much the same way as performative language. At the moment of birth, in answer to the question 'What is it?', the answer is always 'It's a boy' or 'It's a girl'. The use of the pronoun boy or girl transforms the pre-human 'it' into a gendered subject. In this, the first of many performative acts, the body of the child is made culturally intelligible. The pronouncement, 'It's a girl' or 'It's a boy', comes with rules and regulations that pre-exist the child, which the child is expected to follow and obey: 'little boys do this, little girls don't do that', etc. In other words, what seems like an announcement of recognition is in fact a moment of constitution: the 'it' is made a subject (male or female) and thus begins a continuous process of subjectification in which the 'it' is required to conform to culturally intelligible (i.e., socially acceptable) norms of male or femaleness – in this way, the subject is subjected. So, naming me a boy does not reveal my gender identity, it produces it; a production that maps out key aspects of my identity and my social 'destiny'. Moreover, specific patterns of consumption are part of the mapping and 'destiny'.

However, for 'it's a girl' or 'it's a boy' to make sense, it must conform to a structure of cultural intelligibility that already exists (that is, we must already know what it means to say 'it's a girl' or 'it's a boy'). But more than this, the structure of intelligibility demands that such a pronouncement be made; it is an act of conformity to a world that has already agreed to divide humans into male and female on the grounds of certain aspects of biological difference. Each time this happens, the pronouncement is citing previous pronouncements and it is the fact that it is citing these previous pronouncements that give it its authority and validity. This part of Butler's argument draws on Jacques Derrida's extension of Austin's theory of performative language. As Derrida asks, 'Could a performative utterance succeed if its formulation did not repeat a "coded" or iterable utterance, in other words, if the formula I pronounce in order to open a meeting, launch a ship or a marriage were not identifiable as conforming with an iterable model?' (1982: 18). In this way, the power of each pronouncement, why it makes sense, why it has authority and validity and requires conformity, is the weight of previous citations. Moreover, this first citation is the beginning of a continuous process of further citations, as the 'it' is required to conform to the social norms of its assigned gender identity. Our gender identity, therefore, is 'not the product of a choice, but the forcible citation of a norm, one whose complex historicity is indissociable from relations of discipline, regulation, punishment' (Butler, 1993: 232). A variety of discourses, including those from parents, advertising, fashion, educational institutions, the media, will all combine to ensure our conformity to the reiteration and citation of gender norms. In this way, the performance of gender creates the illusion of an already existing gendered self (guaranteed by biology). Sarah Chinn provides an excellent summary of the process, and how it is implicated in learned patterns of consumption,

The naturalizing effects of gender means that gender feels natural – even the understanding that it is performative, that our subjectivities themselves are constructed through its performance, does not make it feel any the less intrinsic. Our identities depend upon successful performance of our genders, and there is an entire cultural arsenal of books, films, television, advertisements, parental injunctions and peer surveillance to make sure those performances are (ideally) unconscious and successful.

(1997: 306–307)

If, as Butler maintains, 'gender reality is created through sustained social performances' (1999: 180): it is acting like a man or a woman that produces gender identities, and specific patterns of consumption are a significant part of the acting that is required. There is not a 'natural self' that performs different identities – a distinction between being and doing. Rather being ('natural self') and doing ('presentation of self') are the same: it is doing masculine things that make a man masculine; men do not have masculinity, they *do* masculinity/masculinities, and part of how it is done is through social practices of consumption. In other words, our gender identities are in part constructed through conforming to learned patterns of consumption. But more than this, the logic of Butler's argument is that all identities are constructed in this way.[6]

NOTES

1 Trentmann (2017: 230) seems to think that Marx believed that alienation was caused by consumption. The opposite is in fact true. It is from work under the capitalist mode of production that alienation derives; consumption is used to lessen its effect, representing an almost hopeless attempt to counter the negative effects of production.

2 As Fine and Leopold point out,

> The concept of emulation (source of the trickle-down effect) … establishes a progressive role for the upper classes in the creation of consumer society. They are seen as the ultimate source of demand, introducing ideas for consumption goods which are passed down through all other strata in society, transformed as they go from luxuries to decencies to basic necessities. There is an implication that the state of idleness made possible by unearned incomes may be warranted by the inventiveness

of those so under-occupied in dreaming up demands for new luxury goods .... The belief that wealth produces 'breeding', which is itself the source of taste and refinement, is therefore used to justify the existence of the social pyramid. But the inequalities of that pyramid are entirely glossed over. (176)

3   An excellent introduction to Romanticism's new way of seeing is the 'Advertisement' (1798) and 'Preface' and 'Appendix' (1802) to the first two editions of *Lyrical Ballads* by William Wordsworth and Samuel Taylor Coleridge. See Wordsworth (2008).

4   Campbell is aware that Romanticism's influence on the development of consumer society is to say the least ironic, especially so, given that its proponents' own perception of what they were doing involved a sense of being against the emerging industrial society in which they lived (see Campbell 1983: 293; 1987: 209). But also consider Romantic poet Robert Southey's attitude to London shops as quoted earlier in this chapter in the section on social emulation.

5   Campbell's theory has a certain resemblance to Jacques Lacan's theory of 'lack'. Lacan argues that we are born into a condition of 'lack' and subsequently spend the rest of our lives trying to overcome this condition. The result is an endless quest in search of an imagined moment of plenitude. Lacan figures this as a search for what he terms l'objet petit a (the object small other); that which is desired but forever out of reach; a lost object, signifying an imaginary moment in time when we were whole. Unable to ever take hold of this object, we console ourselves with displacement strategies and substitute objects. See Storey (2021a).

6   In the sociological classic, *The Presentation of Self in Everyday Life*, Erving Goffman argues that our actions and interactions are a form of performance. That is, he makes a distinction between a natural self (that is singular) and a performed self (that is plural). He gives the example of female students in US colleges in the late 1950s:

> American college girls ... play down their intelligence, skills, and determinativeness when in the presence of datable boys ... These performers are reported to allow their boyfriends to explain things to them tediously that they already know; they conceal proficiency in mathematics from their less able consorts; they lose ping-pong games just before the ending.
>
> (1990: 48)

He quotes a female student making the following complaint: 'At times I resent him! Why isn't he my superior in all ways in which a man should excel so that I could be my natural self? What am I doing here with him, anyhow? Slumming?' (229). She believes that behind her performance of playing dumb is a natural self, engaging in what Goffman calls 'impression management' (85). However, from the perspective of Butler's theory, these performances are performative. The more the male and female students perform in this way, the more this way of performing becomes normative, the more this becomes the way that male and female college students are expected to perform. In other words, by performing in this way, they are helping to reproduce the canon for future citation and reiteration. The female college students were performing a 'regulatory fiction' (Butler 1999: 180). As Butler makes clear, our identity is not the expression of a natural self with which we were born, it is performatively constructed in processes of iteration and citation, which gradually produce and reinforce our sense of identity.

3

EXPLAINING CONSUMPTION

In this chapter, we examine three explanations of how consumption supposedly works: manipulation, communication, and secondary production. The chapter begins with a critical assessment of the Frankfurt School. The section on consumption as communication will then explore the foundational work in sociology of an economist, Thorstein Veblen (working in the USA), and a sociologist, Georg Simmel (working in Germany). This will be followed by a discussion of an influential study on the symbolic use of goods by social anthropologist Mary Douglas and economist Baron Isherwood. The work of the French sociologist Pierre Bourdieu on consumption and its use to mark and maintain social distinctions is discussed in the next section. French cultural theorist Michel de Certeau on consumption as secondary production is the subject of the final section.

CONSUMPTION AS MANIPULATION

The Frankfurt School is the name given to a group of German intellectuals associated with the Institute for Social Research at the University of Frankfurt. The Institute was established in 1923. Following the coming to power of Nazism in Germany in 1933, the Institute moved to New York, becoming a temporary part (until 1949) of the University of Columbia. The experience of life in the US had a profound impact on the school's thinking on consumption. In 1947, Theodor Adorno and Max Horkheimer coined the term 'culture industry' to designate the products and processes of mass culture. The products of the culture industry, they claim,

DOI: 10.4324/9781003224471-3

are marked by two features: cultural homogeneity, 'film, radio and magazines make up a system which is uniform as a whole and in every part ... all mass culture is identical' (1979: 120–121), and predictability:

> As soon as the film begins, it is quite clear how it will end, and who will be rewarded, punished, or forgotten. In light music [popular music], once the trained ear has heard the first notes of the hit song, it can guess what is coming and feel flattered when it does come. (125)

Furthermore, 'Under the regime of the culture industry ... the film leaves no room for imagination or reflection on the part of its audience ... the film forces its *victims* to equate it directly with reality' (353–354; my italics). In a later essay, Adorno elaborates the same theme that the outcomes of consumption are determined by production: 'In all its branches, products which are tailored for consumption by the masses, and which to a great extent determine the nature of that consumption, are manufactured according to plan .... The culture industry intentionally integrates its consumers from above' (1991: 85).

The Frankfurt School maintains that the culture industry, by producing products marked by 'standardisation, stereotype, conservatism, mendacity, manipulated consumer goods' (Lowenthal, 1961: 11), had worked to depoliticize the working class; that is, it had limited its horizon to political and economic goals that could be realized within the oppressive and exploitative framework of capitalist society. Leo Lowenthal contends, 'Whenever revolutionary tendencies show a timid head, they are mitigated and cut short by a false fulfilment of wish-dreams, like wealth, adventure, passionate love, power and sensationalism in general' (ibid.). In short, the culture industry discouraged the 'masses' from thinking beyond the confines of the present. Herbert Marcuse develops this line of argument, to suggest that capitalism, working through the culture industry, promotes an 'ideology of consumerism', which generates false needs,[1] and that these needs work as a mechanism of social control:

> the irresistible output of the entertainment and information industry [the culture industry] carry with them prescribed

attitudes and habits, certain intellectual and emotional reactions which bind the consumers more or less pleasantly to the producers and, through the latter to the whole. The products indoctrinate and manipulate; they promote a false consciousness which is immune against its falsehood ... it becomes a way of life. It is a good way of life – much better than before – and as a good way of life, it militates against qualitative change. Thus emerges a pattern of one-dimensional thought and behaviour in which ideas, aspirations, and objectives that, by their content, transcend the established universe of discourse and action are either repelled or reduced to the terms of this universe.

(2002: 14)

In other words, by supplying the means to certain needs, capitalism, working through the productions of the culture industry, can prevent the formation of more fundamental desires. The inevitable result, or so it is claimed, is that the political imagination of working people is stunted. Work under capitalism stunts the senses; consumption of the products of the culture industry continues the process: 'the escape from everyday drudgery which the whole culture industry promises ... [is a] paradise ... [of] the same old drudgery ... escape ... [is] predesigned to lead back to the starting point. Pleasure promotes the resignation which it ought to help to forget' (Adorno and Horkheimer, 1979: 142). In short, work leads to mass culture; the consumption of mass culture leads back to work. In this way, the Frankfurt School argue, work and leisure under capitalism form a compelling relationship: the effects of the culture industry are guaranteed by the nature of work; the work process secures the effects of the culture industry. The function of the culture industry is therefore, ultimately, to organize leisure time in the same way as capitalist industrialization has organized work time.

Despite its Marxist sophistication, the approach of the Frankfurt School to consumption (especially the consumption of the working class) is, ultimately, a conservative discourse from above (a discourse of 'us' and 'them') on the culture of other people. Moreover, it is a form of analysis that leaves very little room for a critical engagement with consumption, other than one, that is, in which we know all the answers before we ask the questions. For the Frankfurt

School, consumption is passive; what it means and the effects it produces can be explained by a critical understanding of production. It encourages a detailed understanding of the workings of production, while suggesting that a cursory sociological glance will be more than enough to understand the practices of consumption. The latter is understood by an analysis of the former. What is needed is a more complex account. The problem with the mode of analysis advocated by the Frankfurt School is that it addresses only the beginning of the process of consumption. What it describes is better understood, to borrow Stuart Hall's (1996b) phrase, as 'determination by the economic in the first instance' (45). There are economic conditions, and fear of economic reductionism will not remove them. But we cannot simply detail these conditions, to produce an understanding of how these conditions generate a repertoire of commodities; what is also required is an understanding of the many ways in which people select, appropriate, and use these commodities (see Chapters 6 and 7). There also needs to be full recognition that a commodity produced by the culture industries may not have sole access to an individual consumer; first, consumption always occurs in a context (i.e. a social space often containing other people and other commodities, perhaps making counterclaims, or just seeking to undermine the appeal of a rival's products); second, consumers are not blank sheets of paper, but people who come to acts of consumption with a history of other moments of consumption, which may have an impact on current consumption.

Adorno assumes that consumption is always passive, little more than the reception of a single intended meaning. His account of an American situation comedy makes this very clear. It is a story about a young schoolteacher who is both underpaid and continually fined by her school principal. As a result, she is without money and therefore without food. The humour of the storyline consists in her various attempts to secure a meal at the expense of friends and acquaintances. According to Adorno, 'the script implies' that:

> If you are humorous, good natured, quick witted, and charming as she is, do not worry about being paid a starvation wage.... In other words, the script is a shrewd method of promoting adjustment to humiliating conditions by presenting them as

objectively comical and by giving a picture of a person who experiences even her own inadequate position as an object of fun apparently free of any resentment.

(1991: 143–144)

For Adorno, this is the only way an audience can consume the programme. A comment by German playwright Bertolt Brecht points to another way, one that implies a less passive audience. Discussing his own play, *Mother Courage and Her Children*, Brecht suggests, 'Even if Courage learns nothing else at least the audience can, in my view, learn something by observing her' (1978: 229). The same point can be made with reference to the schoolteacher's behaviour. It is only by starting with the assumption that the show dictates its meaning to a passive audience that Adorno can be so certain about how it will be consumed. In Chapter 7, we will examine what happens when we start with different assumptions. Also see discussion of Michel de Certeau in the final section of this chapter.

CONSUMPTION AS COMMUNICATION

Around the turn of the nineteenth century, Thorstein Veblen's writing in 1899 in the US and Georg Simmel's writing in 1903 and 1904 in Germany published work that discussed new patterns of urban middle-class consumption. Both had a profound impact on the development of sociology, especially in terms of our understanding of consumption as a communicative process.

Veblen argues that what he calls the leisure class, as part of its strategy to secure and display its new social position, seeks to present what it has acquired through success in business as if it were something natural to itself. 'Conspicuous consumption' (a term he coined) is the chosen means to communicate this fact to other social classes. He argues against the view that this is little more than a harmless and irrelevant display. According to Veblen, the social display of conspicuous consumption is the very pageant of power; from its prestige grows authority. Moreover, he insists that 'the leisure-class scheme of life ... extends its coercive influence' throughout society (1994: 83–84). 'The leisure class stands at the head of the social structure in point of reputability; and its manner of life and its standards of worth therefore afford the norm of reputability for the community' (84). In this way, the example of the leisure class acts to direct social energies away from productive work and into wasteful displays of conspicuous consumption.

He offers the example of the ways in which the canons of conspicuous consumption exercise a distorting influence over ideals of feminine beauty. The delicate and the diminutive, for example, are promoted to display to the world that the women of the leisure class are far removed from productive work. In this way, women are reduced to symbols of 'vicarious consumption'. Woman is little more than a servant, whose task is to exhibit in a public display her master's economic power. According to Veblen, 'She is useless and expensive, and she is consequently valuable as evidence of pecuniary strength' (149). Women learn to conform to this standard, and men learn to read women's conformity as the very epitome of feminine beauty. Modes of male dress are not exempt from the dictates of the leisure-class canons of decency and good taste. Male apparel must demonstrate the ability to consume without economic restraint. It must also indicate that the wearer is not engaged in productive work. As Veblen explains, 'Elegant dress serves its purpose of elegance not only in that it is expensive, but also because it is the insignia of leisure. It not only shows that the wearer is able to consume a relatively large value, but it argues at the same time that he consumes without producing' (171).[2]

In an essay called 'The Metropolis and Mental Life' (first published in 1903), the German sociologist Georg Simmel identified a similar mode of behaviour in the new distinctive urban culture of Berlin at the turn of the century. Confronted by the perceived anonymity of city life, the new urban middle class used specific patterns of consumption to maintain and display a sense of individuality. As he observed, 'The deepest problems of modern life derive from the claim of the individual to preserve the autonomy and individuality of his existence in the face of overwhelming social forces' (1964: 409). Faced with 'the difficulty of asserting his own personality within the dimensions of metropolitan life' (420), middle-class individuals are 'tempted to adopt the most tendentious peculiarities ... extravagances of mannerism, caprice, and precariousness' (421). Simmel argues that the 'meaning' of such behaviour lies not in its specific content but 'in its form of "being different", of standing out in a striking manner and thereby attracting attention' (ibid.).

Simmel further pursued and elaborated these ideas in an essay on fashion (originally published in 1904). In this essay, he argues that modern urban societies are marked by an increased tension between 'two antagonistic principles', which, he claims, have governed the historical development of the human race – the principles of 'generalization' and 'specialization' (1957: 542). Simmel sees these principles as manifest in two types of individuals, the 'imitative' and the 'teleological'. As he explains, 'The imitator is the passive individual, who believes in social similarity and adapts himself to existing elements; the teleological individual, on the other hand, is ever experimenting, always restlessly striving, and he relies on his own personal conviction' (543). Fashion, driven as it is by a continuous social cycle of imitation and differentiation, is for Simmel an excellent example of these principles in social operation. Moreover, it is a process that depends for its success on the active involvement of both types of individuals, imitative (who follow fashions and thus satisfy their need to adapt) and teleological (who instigate them and thus satisfy their need to innovate). In more general terms, the way fashion as a social practice is said to work is that subordinate groups seek to improve their social status by imitating the dress codes and forms of behaviour of their immediate superordinate group; the superordinate group is then forced to seek new fashions in order to maintain its social difference. As Simmel explains it, 'the fashions of the upper stratum of society are never identical with those of the lower; in fact, they are abandoned by the former as soon as the latter prepares to appropriate them' (ibid.). In this way, he argues, 'Fashion ... is a product of class distinction' (544). It is of course always more than the product; it also has a role to play as producer, in that by a strategy of inclusion and exclusion, fashion helps reproduce social power and privilege by marking and maintaining the social differences and distinctions upon which it in part depends. As Simmel points out, 'fashion ... signifies union with those in the same class, the uniformity of a circle characterized by it, and ... the exclusion of all other groups' (ibid.). It is not the content of fashion that matters, but the social differences it makes visible and helps maintain.

Just as soon as the lower classes begin to copy their style, thereby crossing the line of demarcation the upper classes have drawn and destroying the uniformity of their coherence, the upper classes turn away from this style and adopt a new one, which in turn differentiates them from the masses. (545)

When considering the relevance of the work of Veblen and Simmel for a critical understanding of consumption as it is now practiced in the twenty-first century, we must fully recognize the historical location of their work and the historical problems it was seeking to address. This raises the question, are their critical insights still relevant for an understanding of contemporary practices of consumption? The answer is a qualified yes.[3] In general terms, the practices and motivations they identified, if anything, seem more widespread now than ever before, and this, paradoxically, is the problem. Put simply, people from all social classes seem to now use consumption conspicuously to mark their difference from and similarity to other consumers. Equally, Simmel's general argument about fashion is no longer only applicable to the rich. But there is a problem with simply thinking we can transfer their arguments to the contemporary. Perhaps the most significant is their assumption that modern urban societies have consensual hierarchies of taste, mirroring consensual hierarchies of social class. In other words, those at the bottom or in the middle, it is assumed strive to be like those at the top. This is a very linear model of consumption, which excludes the possibility that classes, other than those at the top, might well choose to compete to be different, or that fashions could originate from both bottom and middle. Both men simply assume that those at the bottom or those in the middle will always seek to emulate those at the top of the class structure. But beyond this, and even more crucially, it is necessary to broaden the scope of who might be involved in practices of conspicuous consumption and of imitation and differentiation. Such activity is no longer limited to social classes. It can also be used to mark differences of, for example, gender, ethnicity, generation, and sexuality.

LiAnne Yu makes an interesting modification to Veblen's argument to understand luxury consumption in China. Instead of conspicuous consumption, which is often used to explain the consumption of luxury items by Chinese consumers, she deploys the term 'conspicuous accomplishment' (2019: 135). As she explains,

'Chinese consumption practices are characterized not by the desire to appear idle and indulgent, but to appear successful through one's personal efforts and hard work. What Chinese consumers seek to display through the symbolism of luxury items is in fact their own capacity for accomplishment' (ibid.).

For Veblen, who was writing about a 'leisure class', what was being communicated was a sense of always having been there; a natural position, unrelated to work or effort. Contrary to this, Yu argues that in China what consumers are seeking to convey is upward mobility without any attempt to hide the effort and work involved. As she explains, 'Among consumers in China, there is no attempt to hide hard work or the fact that one has come from a difficult or humble background. In fact, such narratives of upward mobility and entrepreneurialism are valued over the appearance of idleness' (137). Instead of a leisure class, what we have is a new form of upwardly mobile 'working class'.[4]

In stark contrast to the positions outlined by Veblen and Simmel, Mary Douglas and Baron Isherwood reject the view that 'emulation, envy, and striving to be better than the Joneses are the intentions which fuel consumption' (1996: xxi). Instead of imitation and exclusion, they see consumption as a form of expression, more concerned with 'making visible and stable the categories of culture' (38). According to Douglas and Isherwood, because goods are expressive, they can be used as a symbolic means to communicate with others. As they contend, 'goods are part of a live information system' (xiv). Although 'Goods are neutral, their uses are social; they can be used as fences or bridges' (xv). As they explain, 'As far as keeping a person alive is concerned, food and drink are needed for physical services; but as far as social life is concerned, they are needed for mustering solidarity, attracting support, requiting kindnesses, and this goes for the poor as well as for the rich' (xxi). The symbolic value of objects in the 'information system' is not inherent in the objects themselves. Value is something 'conferred by human judgments' (xxii). To understand the value of one object, it is necessary to locate it in the information system as a whole. Similarly, goods do not communicate by themselves, they communicate 'like flags' (xxiv), and thus require the active agency of human subjects. But as they insist, 'consumption goods are most definitely not mere messages; they constitute the very system itself.

Take them out of human intercourse and you have dismantled the whole thing' (49). In this way, 'Consumption is the very arena in which culture is fought over and licked into shape' (37). As they observe,

> The housewife with her shopping basket arrives home: some things in it she reserves for her household; some for the father, some for the children; others are destined for the special delectation of guests. Whom she invites into her house, what parts of the house she makes available to outsiders, how often, what she offers them for music, food, drink, and conversation, these choices express and generate culture in its general sense.
>
> (ibid.)

Rather than seeing the consumption of goods as 'primarily needed for subsistence [economic theory] plus competitive display [Veblen and Simmel]', they argue that the consumption of goods has a 'double role in providing subsistence and in drawing lines of social relationships' (39). As a mode of communication, 'the essential function of consumption is its capacity to make sense' (40); and thus to 'make and maintain social relationships' (39). Moreover, we must leave behind the 'false distinction' between goods that minister to physical needs (eating and drinking, for example), and those that tender to our more aesthetic inclinations (reading poetry, watching television, for example), because, as they insist, 'all goods carry meaning' (49). Furthermore, 'any choice between goods is the result of, and contributes to, culture' (52). For example, if I invite friends for dinner, the food and drink I serve is not randomly chosen, it is selected because, hopefully, it is not only good to eat and drink, but also because it communicates something about the evening I have planned. I might invite the same friends to a dinner to celebrate a birthday or I might invite them to watch Manchester United in the Champions League, but at each meal, I will serve food and drink that seems appropriate for the occasion. In other words, at each meal, the meaning of the event is partly constructed as meaningful by the food and drink chosen to communicate these different meanings. In this way, what we consume is not marginal to our evening, it is fundamental to the meaning of the event.

Therefore, to fully appreciate consumption as a mode of communication, we must think of it as a language: 'Forget that commodities are good for eating, clothing, and shelter; forget their usefulness and try instead the idea that commodities are good for thinking; treat them as a nonverbal medium for the human creative faculty' (40–41). The practice of consumption is a 'joint production, with fellow consumers, of a universe of values. Consumption uses goods to make firm and visible a particular set of judgments in the fluid processes of classifying persons and events' (41). Consumption is a 'ritual activity' (45) in which people consume to communicate with other consumers, and the shifting accumulations of these acts of consumption constitute the making of culture. What underpins this system and ultimately gives it meaning, what consumption is in the end really communicating, is an underlying cognitive order. As they explain, 'the clue to finding real partitioning among goods must be to trace some underlying partitioning in society' (68).

In an argument that recalls the work of Veblen and Simmel, but is a great deal more sophisticated than both, French sociologist Pierre Bourdieu demonstrates how particular patterns of consumption, generating cultural capital, and are used for purposes of making, marking, and maintaining social distinction. Whereas Douglas and Isherwood see consumption as the neutral underpinning of 'some underlying partitioning in society', Bourdieu maintains that it is a significant area of struggle between and within social classes. Bourdieu's model of consumption, although sharing Douglas and Isherwood's view of consumption as communication, insists that consumption is not a polite conversation about an underlying cognitive order, but a heated argument about class difference and class distinction. He contends that what people consume does not simply reflect distinctions and differences embedded elsewhere, that consumption makes visible, as Douglas and Isherwood suggest, but that consumption is how difference and distinction are produced, maintained, and reproduced. In other words, consumption does not reflect the social order; it helps produce and legitimize it. Like Veblen, he seeks to demonstrate how what dominant classes consume is part of a strategy for hierarchizing social space. However, whereas Veblen was concerned almost exclusively with the leisure class, Bourdieu argues that differences in consumption are always an important aspect in the struggle between dominant and subordinate classes. He shows how arbitrary tastes and arbitrary ways of living are continually transmuted into legitimate taste and the only legitimate way of life. The 'illusion of "natural distinction" is ultimately based on the power of the dominant to impose, by their very existence, a definition of excellence which [is] nothing other than their own way of existing' (1992: 255). In other words, dominant classes seek to impose their own tastes as if these were in fact universal tastes.[5]

Bourdieu's interest is in the processes by which patterns of consumption help to secure and legitimate forms of power and domination that are ultimately rooted in economic inequality. In other words, he argues that although class rule is ultimately economic, the form it takes is cultural; patterns of consumption are used to secure social distinction, the making, marking, and maintaining of social difference. The source of social difference and social power is thus symbolically shifted from the economic field to the field of consumption, making social power appear to be the result of a specific cultural disposition. In this way, the production and reproduction of cultural space help produce and reproduce social space, social power, and class difference. Bourdieu's purpose, therefore, is not to prove the self-evident, that different classes have different patterns of consumption, but to show how consumption (from high art to food on the table) forms a distinct pattern of social distinction, and to identify and interrogate the processes by which the making and maintaining of these distinctions secures and legitimates forms of power and control rooted ultimately in economic inequalities. He is interested not so much in the actual differences, but in how these differences are used by dominant classes as a means of social reproduction. Only by producing a 'barbarous reintegration of aesthetic consumption into the world of ordinary consumption (against which it endlessly defines itself)' (100), will we fully understand the social and political role of consumption. As he maintains, 'one cannot fully understand cultural practices unless "culture", in the restricted, normative sense of ordinary usage, is brought back into "culture" in the anthropological sense, and the elaborated taste for the most refined objects is reconnected with the elementary taste for the flavours of food' (1).

Bourdieu insists that taste is always more than an aesthetic category. As he points out, 'taste classifies, and it classifies the classifier' (6). We are classified by our classifications and classify others by theirs. In this way, he would argue that similar things are happening when I 'value' a holiday destination or a particular mode of dress, is happening when I 'value' a poem by John Clare, a song by Bob Dylan, or an opera by Giacomo Puccini. Such evaluations are never a simple matter of individual taste; consumption operates both to identify and to mark social distinction and to sustain social difference. While such strategies of classification do not in themselves produce social inequalities, the making, marking, and maintaining of them functions to legitimate such inequalities. In this way, taste is a profoundly ideological discourse; it operates as a marker of 'class' (using the term in the double sense to mean both socio-economic category and a particular level of quality). He argues that consumption is, ultimately, 'predisposed ... to fulfil a social function of legitimating social difference' (7).[6]

The consumption of art is for Bourdieu the model for all forms of consumption. At the pinnacle of the hierarchy of taste is the 'pure' aesthetic gaze – a historical invention – with its emphasis on aesthetic distance, and on form over function. Aesthetic distance is in effect the denial of function: it insists on the 'how' and not the 'what'. It is analogous to the difference between judging a meal good because it was economically priced and filling, and judging a meal good based on how it was served, where it was served, etc. The 'pure' aesthetic gaze emerges with the emergence of the cultural field (in which texts and practices are divided into culture and mass culture).[7] One in effect guarantees the other. Bourdieu sees the art museum as the institutionalization of the aesthetic gaze and the cultural field. Once inside the museum art loses all prior functions (except that of being art) and becomes pure form: 'Though originally subordinated to quite different or even incompatible functions (crucifix and fetish, Pieta and still life), these juxtaposed works tacitly demand attention to form rather than function, technique rather than theme' (30). For example, an advertisement for soup displayed in an art gallery becomes an example of the aesthetic, whereas the same advertisement in a magazine is an example of the commercial. The effect of the distinction is to produce 'a sort of ontological promotion akin to a transubstantiation' (6). It is the institutionalization of such distinctions that produces what he calls the 'ideology of natural taste', the view that genuine 'appreciation' can only be attained by an instinctively gifted minority armed against the mediocrity of the masses. Ortega y Gasset makes the point with precision: 'art helps the "best" to know and recognise one another in the greyness of the multitude and to learn their mission, which is to be few in number and to have to fight against the multitude' (quoted in Bourdieu, 1992: 31; see also Storey, 2003).[8]

As Bourdieu points out, 'it is not easy to describe the "pure" gaze without also describing the naive gaze which it defines itself against' (32). The naive gaze is of course the gaze of the popular aesthetic:

> The affirmation of continuity between art and life, which implies the subordination of form to function ... a refusal of the refusal which is the starting point of the high aesthetic, i.e., the clear cut separation of ordinary dispositions from the specially aesthetic disposition. (32)

The relation between the pure and the popular aesthetic is needless to say not one of equality, but a relation of dominant and dominated. The popular aesthetic, in its stress on function over form, is necessarily contingent and pluralistic, contrary, and in deference to the absolute insistence of the supposed transcendent universality of the pure aesthetic. Bourdieu sees the two aesthetics as articulating the two separate but related realms of necessity and freedom. Without the required cultural capital to decipher the 'code' of art, people are made socially vulnerable to the condescension of those who do have cultural capital. What is social is presented as innate, and, in turn, used to justify what is social. Like other ideological strategies, 'The ideology of natural taste owes its plausibility and its efficacy to the fact that ... it naturalises real differences, converting differences in the mode of acquisition of culture into differences of nature' (68). Aesthetic relations thus mimic and help reproduce social relations of power. As Bourdieu observes,

> Aesthetic intolerance can be terribly violent.... The most intol-
> erable thing for those who regard themselves as the possessors
> of legitimate culture is the sacrilegious reuniting of tastes which
> taste dictates shall be separated. This means that the games of
> artists and aesthetes and their struggles for the monopoly of
> artistic legitimacy are less innocent than they seem. At stake in
> every struggle over art there is also the imposition of an art of
> living, that is, the transmutation of an arbitrary way of living
> into the legitimate way of life which casts every other way of
> living into arbitrariness. (57)

Bourdieu's work on consumption is underpinned by his view of
education. Rather than being a means to lessen inequality, it functions to legitimate it. He argues that the education system fulfils
a quite specific social and political function: that is, to legitimate
social inequalities which exist prior to its operations. It achieves
this by transforming social differences into academic differences
and presenting these differences as if they were 'grounded in
nature' (387). The cultural tastes of dominant classes are given
institutional form, and then, with deft ideological sleight of hand,
their taste for this institutionalized culture (i.e., their own) is
held up as evidence of their cultural, and, ultimately, their social,
superiority. In this way, social distinction is generated by learned
patterns of consumption that are internalized as 'natural' cultural
preferences and interpreted and mobilized as evidence of 'natural'
cultural competences, which are, ultimately, used to justify forms
of class domination. To fully understand this, we need to understand how Bourdieu distinguishes between three types of capital –
economic, social, and cultural. In capitalist societies, economic
capital in the form of money, property, etc. is able to buy access
to cultural and social capital. Hierarchies openly based on the
accumulation of economic capital are vulnerable to challenge.
Cultural and social capital can conceal and legitimate economic
domination by reproducing it in the form of cultural and social
hierarchies. One of the great strengths of Bourdieu's work on
consumption is that, together with the introduction of invaluable
concepts such as cultural capital and social distinction, it makes
visible political practices that are in the very fabric of everyday
life but are rarely seen as political at all.[9]

CONSUMPTION AS POACHING

The French cultural theorist Michel de Certeau also interrogates the term 'consumer', to reveal the activities that are often concealed within the act of consumption or what he prefers to call 'secondary production' (2019: 603). Consumption, as he says, 'is devious, it is dispersed, but it insinuates itself everywhere, silently and almost invisibly, because it does not manifest itself through its own products, but rather through its ways of using the products imposed by a dominant economic order' (602). For de Certeau, the field of consumption is a site of continual conflict (silent and almost invisibly) between the 'strategy' of imposition (production) and the 'tactics' of use (consumption or 'secondary production'). The sociologist must be continually alert to 'the difference or similarity between ... production ... and ... secondary production hidden in the process of ... utilisation' (603). He characterizes the active consumption of texts as 'poaching': 'readers are travellers: they move across lands belonging to someone else, like nomads poaching their way across the fields they did not write' (1984: 174). The idea of reading as poaching is clearly a rejection of any theoretical position that assumes that the 'message' of a text is something which is imposed on a reader. Such approaches, he argues, are based on a fundamental misunderstanding of the processes of consumption. It is a 'misunderstanding [which] assumes that "assimilating" necessarily, means "becoming similar to" what one absorbs, and not "making something similar" to what one is, making it one's own, appropriating or reappropriating it' (166). In *Cultural Theory and Popular Culture* (Storey, 2019: 227), there is a photo of a sculpture from Qingdao in China. It shows a variety of Chinese citizens entering a Coca-Cola house and leaving it as little Coca-Cola people, all exactly the same. The assumption behind the artwork is that consuming American culture Americanizes Chinese citizens. In other words, we become what we consume. This is structure without agency (and is reminiscent of Adorno as discussed earlier). To repeat de Certeau's point, and it is worth repeating, it is a 'misunderstanding [which] assumes that "assimilating" necessarily, means "becoming similar to" what one absorbs, and not "making something similar" to what one is, making it one's own, appropriating or reappropriating it' (1984: 166). For example, in China, Coca-Cola is boiled with fresh ginger to make a drink which is said to ease the common cold, but which can also be enjoyed simply as a tasty hot beverage – an example of appropriation, not Americanization.

Acts of poaching are always in potential conflict with the 'scriptural economy' (131–176) of textual producers and those institutional voices (teachers, lecturers, etc.) who, through an insistence on the authority of authorial and/or textual meaning, work to limit and confine the production and circulation of 'un-authorized' meanings. In this way, de Certeau's notion of poaching is a challenge to traditional models of reading, in which the purpose of reading is the passive reception of authorial and/or textual intent: that is, models of reading in which reading is reduced to a question of being 'right' or 'wrong' (which can be confirmed by teacher or lecturer, etc.). He makes an interesting observation about how the notion of a text containing a hidden meaning, available only to the trained critic, may help sustain certain relationships of power in matters of pedagogy and academic life:

> This fiction condemns consumers to subjection because they are always going to be guilty of infidelity or ignorance when confronted by the mute "riches" of the treasury…. The fiction of the "treasury" hidden in the work, a sort of strong-box full of meaning, is obviously not based on the productivity of the reader, but on the social institution that overdetermines his relation with the text. Reading is as it were overprinted by a relationship of forces (between teachers and pupils …) whose instrument it becomes. (171)

This may in turn produce a teaching practice in which 'students … are scornfully driven back or cleverly coaxed back to the meaning "accepted" by their teachers' (172). This is often informed by what we might call 'object determinism': the view that the value and meaning of something is inherent in the thing itself. This position can lead to a way of working in which certain texts and practices are prejudged to be beneath the legitimate concerns of the academic gaze. Against this way of thinking, I would contend that what really matters is not the object of study, but how the object is studied. Moreover, such academic condescension has no productive place in the sociological study of consumption.

NOTES

1 For an anthropological critique of the notion of 'true' and 'false' needs, see Marshall Sahlins (1976).

2 The British Conservative MP Jacob Rees-Mogg presents a contemporary example of someone cryogenically trapped in leisure-class canons of decency and good taste.

3 Frank Trentmann, working with a rather strange logic, seems to think that because Veblen was writing 'at a time when people spent more on clothing than on housing' (2017: 339), this makes his approach no longer valid. Trentmann rather patronizingly dismisses those who still see value in Veblen's work as 'theorists ... devoted to the consumer as a shopper buying another branded handbag' (ibid.). This reveals a real failure to understand work on consumption in sociology and cultural studies.

4 But there are clear limits to displays of conspicuous accomplishment. In March 2021, about 4,000 accounts, showing short videos featuring 'elites with rags-to-riches stories', were removed from Douyin (the Chinese original of TikTok) for 'irrational wealth flaunting' and 'money worship' (https://www.scmp.com/tech/big-tech/article/3123613/tiktok-sister-app-douyin-removes-thousands-accounts-flaunting-wealth; accessed 17/12/21).

5 There is a certain similarity with what Marx and Engels said about class power: 'The ruling class ... is compelled ... to represent its interest as the common interest of all the members of society ... to give its ideas the form of universality, and represent them as the only rational, universally valid ones' (2019: 55).

6 Manisha Anantharaman gives the example of middle-class professionals in Bangalore in India taking up cycling to demonstrate a commitment to the environment. But to distinguish themselves from those who have no choice but to cycle, they use expensive western bikes and equipment. In this way, they change the meaning of the practice of cycling. As one respondent made clear: 'It helps that these bicycles are expensive ... [letting] people around them know that they can buy a car if they want to' (quoted in Middlemiss 2018: 129–130). For a discussion, using Bourdieu, of environmental activist and bicycles, see Horton (2003).

7 For a discussion of the invention of this division, see Storey (2003; 2010).

8 As a schoolchild, you may have read the *Sneetches* by Dr Seuss. It tells a story very similar to Bourdieu's theoretical account, in which changes are made in order to make, mark, and maintain social distinction. The utopian ending depicts a post-class society.

9 It is sometimes claimed that Bourdieu's theory of consumption as the making and marking of distinction is in some fundamental way undermined

by what are called 'cultural omnivores', elite groups who consume across the continuum between high and popular culture. Put simply, it is argued that because elites consume popular culture, Bourdieu's argument is now less valid. Rather than dispute Bourdieu's findings, the idea of the cultural omnivore confirms them. The cultural omnivore does not signal the end of class society, and consumption as class reproduction, only that one of its modes of generation has changed. He understood that the dominant class were able to derive cultural capital from popular culture. It was a matter of how it was consumed. Careful selection and curation of what comes from 'below' further confirms their ability to define what is of value. For a discussion of Bourdieu and cultural omnivores, see Storey (2003).

SUSTAINABLE CONSUMPTION AND CAPITALIST CONSUMERISM

In this chapter, we explore the tensions between capitalism and the idea of sustainable consumption. This will involve what might seem at times a rather rambling discussion of consuming sustainably, capitalist consumer society, advertising, the Anthropocene, and the Capitalocene. The issues are complex; therefore, it is necessary to cover a lot of ground, changing theoretical and historical locations, in order to make clear the connection between consumption, capitalism, and the climate emergency.

CONSUMING SUSTAINABLY

To talk of consumption is for some people to identify a problem. Although it is true that ever-expanding consumption will sooner or later encounter the limited resources of a finite planet, it is also true that many people in the world today, perhaps up to three billion, are unable to consume enough. The limits they encounter are political and social. Therefore, addressing the problem of consumption is not just a question of consume less, it is also a matter of consume more equitably. As Tim Jackson points out, 'The poorest half of the world's population earn less than 7 per cent of the total income. The top 1 per cent by contrast earn about 20 per cent of global income and own almost half of global wealth' (2017: 5). The figures on global inequality are simply quite staggering: 'eighty-five people control as much wealth as half the world's population' (Klein, 2015: 123). 'The eighty richest individuals in the world have a combined income higher than 416 million poorest' (Bonneuil and Fressoz, 2017: 70). Moreover, inequality is increasing. 'In

DOI: 10.4324/9781003224471-4

the space of less than half a century the richest 1 per cent of the population have more than doubled their income share. Income inequality within developing countries increased by 11 per cent in the last two decades. Even within the advanced economies, inequality is 9 per cent higher than it was 20 years ago' (6). As Raj Patel told Naomi Klein, 'The US has more food than it knows what to do with, and still 50 million people are food insecure' (Klein, 2015: 135). The UK is usually regarded as the fifth richest country in the world and yet, according to the House of Commons Library, it is home to 2,200 food banks where people must go for food they cannot afford to buy.[1]

Put simply, the rich consume more than the poor and therefore have a greater negative impact on the environment. The richest 10 per cent of the global population are responsible for 50 per cent of carbon emissions, while the poorest 50 per cent are responsible for only 10 per cent (Middlemiss, 2018: 23). Princeton University's Carbon Mitigation Initiative has estimated that around 6 per cent of the richest people on the planet are responsible for around 50 per cent of all global emissions (see Klein, 2015: 114). As Klein explains, 'This is why the persistent positing of population control as a solution to climate change is a distraction and moral dead end …. [T]he most significant cause of rising emissions is not the reproductive behaviour of the poor but the consumer behaviours of the rich' (2015: 114).[2]

Sustainable consumption is the idea that consumption can be managed to deal with the climate emergency. It usually identifies changes in individual consumption as the solution to the problem. While it is true that we can all contribute, the notion that the problem was caused by the consumption practices of individuals is deeply misleading. Deflection is a common strategy in which problems derived from the capitalist system are presented as the responsibility of individuals. Finis Dunaway offers a wonderful summary of this argument, 'The answer to pollution … [has] nothing to do with power, politics or production decisions; it [is] simply a matter of how individuals [act] in their daily lives' (quoted in Mann, 2021: 60). The corporate polluters, and their heavily sponsored experts, what Michael E Mann calls 'all-purpose deniers-for-hire' (2021: 16), part of 'the fossil-fuel-funded climate-change denial machine' (41), have 'masterfully executed a deflection campaign – inspired by those of the gun lobby, the tobacco industry, and the beverage companies – aimed at shifting responsibility from corporations to individuals' (3).[3] Various individual solutions are canvassed as the answer to the climate emergency, including buy a bicycle, stop flying, and go vegan. While all of these have their obvious merits, they alone will not end the crisis. This is not to say that individual action is unimportant. It can raise awareness and contribute to radical change, but it cannot solve the problem. Education and environmental literacy are obviously important, as are individual consumer choices, but without fundamental change to how capitalism encourages and engages in plundering and pollution, we will not address the climate emergency.

Capitalism depends on growth and endless growth threatens the life of the planet and our existence on it. It is a system in which capital goes in search of the means to make more capital. The fantasy of perpetual growth is that it produces wealth for the few that will eventually 'trickle down' to the many. But 'eventually' is a lot like the horizon, always in the distance. Put simply, growth does not reduce poverty: 'Despite phenomenal growth in recent decades, there are 40 million poor in the US, and 11 million in the UK – 12 percent and 17 percent of the population respectively – the same share as in the 1970s' (Kallis et al., 2020: 120). We should therefore not be surprised that 'The poorest 60 percent of humanity receive only 5 percent of all new income generated by global growth' (121). Moreover, 'Degrowth is not forced deprivation, but an aspiration to secure enough for everyone to live with dignity and without fear; to experience friendship, love, and health; to be able to give and receive care; and to enjoy leisure and nature' (18–19). Work less, repair, share and reuse more. These are all admirable things to do, but on their own, they will not reverse the climate crisis. What is necessary is a change in how things are produced – a change in the mode of production. Consuming less is obviously part of the solution. But to present this as *the* solution is deeply misleading.

CAPITALIST CONSUMER SOCIETY

As Marx observes in the opening sentence of *Capital*, 'The wealth of societies in which the capitalist mode of production prevails appears as an immense collection of commodities' (1976a: 125).

When these commodities become central to how a society under-stands itself and increasingly help organize how its citizens see and interact with each other through a language of consumerism, we have a capitalist consumer society. Consumption is no longer just something to do to survive; it becomes a sign of our membership of society. Instead of social identity being defined in terms of what we produce, it increasingly becomes a manifestation of what and how we consume (see Chapter 2).

Historians argue over when it is possible to speak of a capital-ist consumer society. Although modern and contemporary con-sumption is now established as a field of critical enquiry, attention to early modern consumption is still in its preliminary stages. Ann Bermingham suggests that one of the reasons for this is to be found in a version of history made popular by some dominant versions of recent theory; that is, the claim that consumer society is a product of late capitalism. Against this view, Bermingham argues the case for locating the birth of consumer society in the seventeenth century. As she points out, the coming dominance of capitalism witnessed not only an expansion of production, but also a rapid growth in consumption. Moreover, the neglect of consumption in our understanding of these historical changes, she maintains, is a direct consequence of the influence of 'theo-rists of modernism [who] have assigned consumer society to the late twentieth century' (1995: 3). She particularly has in mind Fredric Jameson (1984). Bermingham insists that we must reject the notion that consumer society is simply a phase of late capi-talism and instead see it as 'intrinsic to all phases of capitalism, even the earliest' (4). However, she does not argue that capital-ist consumer society is a monolithic entity, unchanging since its inception in the seventeenth century.

Bermingham is among a growing body of historians who have sought to establish the view that a capitalist consumer society first appears in the seventeenth century. Another influential body of work in historical scholarship has made the argument that it is to the eighteenth century that we should look for the origins of con-sumerism. JH Plumb, for example, asserts with great confidence that, 'During the eighteenth century extraordinary economic and social changes swept through Britain and brought into being the first society dedicated to ever-expanding consumption based on industrial production' (1982: 316). In similar fashion, Neil McKendrick, John Brewer, and JH Plumb claim with conviction, 'There was a consumer revolution in eighteenth-century England' (1982: 1). As they explain,

> More men and women than ever before in human history enjoyed the experience of acquiring material possessions. Objects which for centuries had been the privileged possessions of the rich came, within the space of a few generations, to be within the reach of a larger part of society than ever before, and, for the first time, to be within the legitimate aspirations of almost all of it.
>
> (ibid.)

The consumer revolution of the eighteenth century was the result, they claim, of changes in ways of thinking, changes in retail skills, and changes in economic prosperity across all classes. McKendrick claims 'that consumer behaviour was so rampant and the acceptance of commercial attitudes so pervasive that no one … should doubt that the first of the world's consumer societies had unmistakably emerged [in England] by 1800' (1982: 13). Whether we think it begins in the seventeenth or eighteenth centuries, what is clear is that capitalist consumer society has a longer history than many accounts of it suggest.[4]

SELLING CAPITALISM

Selling capitalism has always involved the idea of selling new consumer identities. As we have discussed at several points in this book, there is a clear and complex relationship between consumption and identity formation. The development of a capitalist consumer society is a key moment in this relationship. Writing in 1747, Richard Campbell mocked those who sought to hide their true selves behind their chosen patterns of consumption.

> There are Numbers of Beings in about this Metropolis who have no other identical Existence than what the Taylor, Milliner, and Perriwig-Maker bestow upon them. Strip them of these Distinctions, and they are quite a different Species of Beings;

have no more Relation to their dressed selves, than they have to the Great Mogul, and are insignificant in Society as Punch, deprived of his moving Wires, and hung up upon a Peg.

(quoted in McKendrick, 1982: 51; capitals in original)

What makes this different from later positions on consumption and identity (see, for example, the discussion of Judith Butler in Chapter 2), is the very idea of a true self that can be disguised and concealed. These accounts of identity and consumption argue, as we have already noted, that we are in part what we consume; identity is not an essence to be dressed in particular ways, it is something we become and continue to become; identity is not what we are but what we are becoming and dressing in a particular way may form part of this process. Stuart Ewen quotes the psychologist Floyd Henry Allport (writing in 1924), who argues that 'our consciousness of ourselves is largely a reflection of the consciousness which others have of us .... My idea of myself is rather my own idea of my neighbour's view of me' (quoted in Ewen, 1976: 34). Advertising plays on this notion of the self by locating the products it advertises in a world where self is continually under the watchful gaze of others, and the only way to be sure that we can successfully withstand such scrutiny is by using one of the products offered to us to purchase. A key moment in this connection between capitalism and identity occurs with the development of the department store in the nineteenth century. The Swiss historian Philippe Perrot describes the impact of the department store in France as dramatic: it 'brought about the psychological "take off" of the desire for consumption in the modern sense, the extended socialisation of needs' (quoted in Laermans, 1993: 80).

By the close of the nineteenth century, the department store was a familiar feature of city shopping; for example, the Bon Marche in Paris, Harrods in London, Kendals in Manchester, Lewis's in Liverpool, Bainbridge's in Newcastle upon Tyne, Macy's in New York, Wanamaker's in Philadelphia. As Rachel Bowlby explains,

Within a very short period, department stores had been established as one of the outstanding institutions in the economic and social life of the late nineteenth century; and together with advertising, which was also expanding rapidly, they marked the beginning of present-day consumer society.

(1985: 3)

The department store brought into being many of the aspects of shopping we now take for granted. For example, as Bowlby also points out,

> The principle of *entrée libre* or open entry did away with what had previously been a moral equation between entering a shop and making a purchase. At the same time, a fixed price policy, supported by clear labelling, put an end to the convention of bargaining which focused attention on shopping as paying. Assistants in department stores received commissions on sales, so were inclined to be flattering rather than argumentative: the customer was now to be waited on rather than negotiated with and money, in appearance, was not part of the exchange (particularly since paying in fact took place in a separate part of the store). People could now come and go, to look and dream, perchance to buy, and shopping became a new bourgeois leisure activity – a way of pleasantly passing the time, like going to a play or visiting a museum. (3–4)

In this way, the discourse of commerce had shifted from an insistence on the 'immediate purchase of particular items' to an attempt to generate and provoke the 'arousal of free-floating desire' (Williams, 1982: 67). In other words, with the advent of the department store, shopping became detached from buying and with this development came the pleasure of looking, with 'just looking' entering for the first time the vocabulary of shopping.[5] The idea is captured wonderfully in the music-hall song, 'Let's Go Shopping':

> Shopping's a pastime simply sublime,
> Nothing to spend but a real good time,
> Examining every pretty thing that the shopmen
> politely display.
> That looks neat! Awf'lly nice! Simply sweet!
> What's the price? Thank you, we'll call another day.
> (quoted in Trentmann, 2017: 201)

As Rudi Laermans observes, 'The early department stores pioneered the transformation of traditional customers into modern consumers and of "just merchandise" into spectacular "commodity signs" or "symbolic goods". Thus, they laid the cornerstones of a culture we still inhabit' (1993: 94). Michael B Miller makes a similar point, with specific reference to France, but generalizable to other areas of Western Europe and North America, the department store did not simply reflect changing consumer practices, it actively and powerfully contributed to them. 'Far more than a mirror of bourgeois culture in France, the Bon Marche gave shape and definition to the very meaning of the concept of a bourgeois way of life' (1981: 182). The department store gave embodiment to this way of life; its catalogues operated as a 'cultural primer', telling readers who wanted this way of life, and these specific identities, 'how they should dress, how they should furnish their home, and how they should spend their leisure time' (183). In this way, the department store promoted the idea that identity was something that could be purchased. Stuart Ewen and Elizabeth Ewen call this possibility 'the commercialization of the self' (1982: 215). In other words, the production of the capitalist subject necessary for the reproduction of the system.

Although the department store was a very visible feature in what became known as mass consumption, it was not, however, the main source of these developments. Shopping more generally grew very rapidly in the nineteenth century, quickly becoming not just a means to satisfy needs but redefined as a popular leisure activity. As Western Europe urbanized, it is in this period that people are first described as shoppers. Trentmann names 'the pedlar, the market hall and the co-operative shop [as] equally creative responses to the growing demands of urban populations' (2017: 191). As he points out,

> The big stores rang up sales, but so did a host of rivals, from pedlars to the co-operative shop. In Western Europe in 1914, department stores controlled less than 3 per cent of the retail trade; in the United States it was slightly more. The stores rarely reached 10 per cent of all clothes and furniture sold. The competitors were not asleep. Small shops multiplied. (205)

In 1914 co-operative shops 'controlled 8 per cent of all retail sales in Britain, three times that of the department stores' (206). But not all these developments were pulling in the same direction. Whereas the department store represented a celebration of the capitalist market, the co-operative shop was a challenge, a reformist alternative to the imperative that commodities and profit represent the ultimate good.

Advertising is fundamental to these changes. As Marx observed, each capitalist demands 'that his workers should save, but only *his own*, because they stand to him as workers; but by no means the remaining *world of workers*, for these stand towards him as consumers. In spite of all "pious" speeches he therefore searches for means to spur them on to consumption, to give his wares new charms, to inspire them with new needs by constant chatter etc.' (1976a: 287; italics in original). Marx would be quite amazed by how the need for 'new charms' and 'constant chatter' has developed into the very powerful industry of advertising. The 'chatter' has become very sophisticated. It had come to dominate most TV channels. For example, 41 per cent of primetime television in the US consists of commercials; in Australia, they take up 13 minutes in every hour; while in the UK, the average viewer is exposed to 48 commercials a day (Lewis, 2013: 64–65). Even when not watching television, it is difficult to escape advertising: we encounter it in sponsorship and product placement and on billboards and other forms of signage, on the Internet and radio, in magazines and newspapers, in the post and on our mobile phones, and it is woven into the narratives of feature films and worn by sporting heroes in the stadiums it names. It has become a very powerful industry indeed. In 2018, $163 billion was spent on radio and print and television ads by the top 200 advertising companies in the US (Hudson and Hudson, 2021: 73).

As we noted in Chapter 1, commodity fetishism hides from sight and understanding the social relations of production. But there is another way in which we might think of the fetishism of commodities. This involves the role played by advertising in their circulation. Advertising takes the 'material shell' of a commodity (Marx, 1976a: 167) and seeks to add signification to utility to increase sales. It transforms the commodity into a fetish, imbued with magical power to make its consumption bring about attractiveness, security, freedom, and desire. Elsewhere (Storey, 2021a) I have discussed how since the 1990s certain non-electric vehicles have been fetishized in adverts; presented on empty roads and deserted landscapes, as if magically existing in harmony with nature and space. This mode of advertising represents a response to the growing body of negative publicity that petrol and diesel car ownership has attracted (especially in terms of pollution and road congestion). To prevent this publicity from having an adverse effect on car sales, these criticisms must be countered. To confront them in a direct way would always run the risk of allowing the criticisms to come between the car being advertised and any potential buyer. Therefore, showing petrol and diesel cars magically in both nature (unpolluted) and space (uncongested) confronts the claims without the risk of giving them a dangerous and unnecessary visibility. In this way, the criticisms are answered without the questions themselves having been formally posed. The emphasis placed on nature and space is, therefore, a response to the twin questions (which remain unasked in the advertisements themselves but exist in the assumptions that organize the adverts): does buying a car increase both pollution and road congestion? The answer given, without the question being asked, is that these cars, as if by magic, neither pollute nor contribute to, or experience, road congestion.

Advertising is not a mechanism to name what is missing. It is not as if there is a lack which advertising then identifies, pointing to products which will satisfy our needs; rather it is the advertising's staging of fantasy which produces and nurtures desire. According to Slavoj Žižek, rather than fulfilling desire, fantasy is the staging of desire. As he explains,

> [W]hat the fantasy stages is not a scene in which our desire is fulfilled, fully satisfied, but on the contrary, a scene that realises, stages, the desire as such. The fundamental point of psychoanalysis is that desire is not something given in advance, but something that has to be constructed – and it is precisely the role of fantasy to give the coordinates of the subject's desire, to specify its object, to locate the position the subject assumes in it. It is only through fantasy that the subject is constituted as desiring: through fantasy, we learn how to desire.
>
> (2019: 436)

In this way, then, 'fantasy space functions as an empty surface, a kind of screen for the projection of desires' (437). So, while advertising always seems to need lack, we should not see it as a passive follower of something missing. Rather than lack producing desire, we could think instead about how desire produces lack. To paraphrase Michel Foucault on power, we should see desire as productive – it does not just lack something, it brings something into existence; it is not simply driven by what is absent, it is a force that makes something present.[6] What I am suggesting is that it is advertising that produces desire, which, in turn, makes visible what we think we lack. In other words, adverts work not as the end point of desire, but as a point where desire begins to be realized. It teaches desire not for itself but as a new way of seeing the world and all the things we 'lack'. As Hudson and Hudson ask, 'Does the running shoe – which on the surface is just a more or less functional assemblage of rubber and textiles – actually connect me to performances, resolve, determination, fashion, celebrity or athleticism, as the marketers would have it? Or does it connect me to the poverty of the seamstress and the toxicity of petrochemical refining?' (2021: 143). Advertising has no intention to take us beneath the material shell of a commodity, where we might discover exploitation and environmental damage; rather, it dresses it in dreams and desires, things we can be because of consumption. Capitalism does not satisfy our fantasies; it needs them continually articulated to reproduce itself.

Advertising is more than a cheerleader for consumer capitalism; it is fundamental to its progress and profitability. This is Lefebvre's point when he writes of what he calls 'the persuasive ideology of consumption' (2002: 78) under which people are 'programmed' to consume. We are told what to buy but most of all we are told to buy. As he explains, 'The publicity that was intended to promote consumption is the first of consumer goods' (105). This ideology has a dual purpose: it promotes specific objects, and it promotes a particular way of life. Through it 'we are told how to live better, how to dress fashionably, how to decorate your house, in short how to exist; you are totally and thoroughly programmed' (107). Therefore, although the bureaucratically controlled structure of consumption may never quite eliminate human agency, it seems to remain the case, according to Lefebvre, that we are 'totally and thoroughly programmed' (ibid.). We do not have to share Lefebvre's rather dogmatic pessimism to recognize the dual purpose of advertising. Individual adverts seek to sell commodities, but advertising more generally helps to sell a way of life – capitalist consumer society. It seeks to establish a particular control over what is important in life. It educates the desire to consume. While not wishing to suggest that it is always successful and that we are little more than cultural dupes, through a process of persuasion and manipulation, advertising seeks to regulate and organize the capitalist marketplace. It is everywhere and nowhere and everywhere it tells the same story: buy this and life will be better.[7] As we have noted, for every problem identified by advertising, there are commodity solutions. In telling this story, it tells another: capitalism is a mode of production that can guarantee happiness for everyone. Do not worry if this does not yet appear to be the case; keep buying, as the 'good life' is just over the counter.

Therefore, to be clear, capitalist consumer society is not the creation of our desire to consume; it is the outcome of capitalism's need to sell what it produces. Capitalist production needs mass consumption. As Marx points out, capitalist consumer society is the result of both production and consumption.

> Production mediates consumption; it creates the latter's material; without it, consumption would lack an object. But consumption also mediates production, in that it alone creates for the products the subject for whom they are products. The product only obtains its 'last finish' in consumption …. Without production no consumption; without consumption no production'.
>
> (1973: 91, 93)

Capitalist consumerism is the ideology that seeks to match consumption with production by convincing us, now redefined as consumers rather than citizens, that consuming commodities is what identifies us as civilized human beings and that every problem and every desire has a commodity solution. The success of capitalism depends on encouraging people to identify as consumers, who are persuaded to think that we are exactly like the self-interested people required by the system. In other words, capitalism does not work to meet our needs; it seeks to convince us to work for its continued reproduction. Therefore, capitalism is not successful because of some key evolutionary feature of human nature. If this were true, why did it take so long for the system to arrive? Our human journey began about 300,000 years ago, while capitalism is at most 500 years old. Almost 99 per cent of human history does not include capitalism. To make the evolutionary claim about human nature is to engage in lazy ahistorical mode of thought. Framing it in this way makes it a problem of individuals. But the fact the system requires consumption for its very existence should make us pause at such an analysis. A system that rewards self-interest will inevitably produce and reproduce self-interest. What we will see is not the manifestation of human nature, but the framing and shaping of human action in ways which meet the needs of the system. The source of capitalist consumer society is not in our heads but is the result of the development of a particular mode of production, with all its greed and irresponsibility. If it was our human nature that drove consumption, capitalism would not have to work so very hard to ensure we continue to consume.

THE ANTHROPOCENE

The Anthropocene is a term said to have been coined by ecologist Eugene Stoermer in the 1980s (see Ellis, 2018; Purdy, 2015).[8] It is the name for a new moment in geological time, the age of humans. As Erle C Ellis explains,

> The history of your planet and your role in it is being rewritten to include a new chapter; a chapter in which you play a leading role. We humans, the Anthropos, have so greatly altered Earth's functioning that scientists now propose to recognise this with a new interval of geologic time: the Anthropocene.
>
> (2018: xv)

Although the term had been around since the 1980s, it was announced to the world in 2000 by the Nobel-prize winning atmospheric chemist Paul Crutzen. It is from this point on that it began its discursive circulation from science to the humanities and then to the media and beyond. Like concepts such as postmodernism and globalization, the Anthropocene has broken free of its academic confines and entered the conversations of the 'general reader'. According to Jason W Moore, 'no other socio-ecological concept has so gripped popular attention' (2016a: 3).

Negative human impact on the planet has been enormous, including polluting it, depleting the ozone layer, changing the climate, acidifying the oceans, destroying forests and other natural habitats, and causing the mass extinction of species. While all of this is undoubtedly true, we must, however, be very careful who we include when we use 'we' and 'our' to identify the source of responsibility. Are we all equally to blame? This might be a convenient fiction for the big fossil fuel corporations, but is it something we should accept? Who is the Anthropos? The answer implied, and sometimes explicit in the narrative of the Anthropocene, is that we are all equally, if unwittingly, responsible for the negative human impact on the planet. As historians Christophe Bonneuil and Jean-Baptiste Fressoz explain,

> There is already an official narrative of the Anthropocene: 'we', the human species, unconsciously destroyed nature to the point of hijacking the Earth system into a new geological epoch. In the late twentieth century, a handful of Earth system scientists finally opened our eyes. So now we know; now we are aware of the global consequences of human action.
>
> (2017: xii)

The concept of the Anthropos tends to reduce humanity to a single actor who is uniformly responsible for the climate emergency. In this way, the concept tends to hide the huge differences that exist between people, producing an argument in which we are all asked to take responsibility for the actions of a wealthy minority. But, for example, again to quote Bonneuil and Fressoz, 'An average American ... consumes thirty-two times more resources and energy than an average Kenyan. A new human being born on Earth will have a carbon footprint a thousand times greater if she is born into a rich family in a rich country, than into a poor family in a poor country' (70).

The concept of Anthropocene not only asks us all to take responsibility for our negative impact on the planet, but it also wants to insist that for too long we looked the other way. But 'We should not act as astonished ingenues who suddenly discover they are transforming the planet: the entrepreneurs of the industrial revolution who brought us into the Anthropocene actively willed this new epoch and shaped it' (xi). As Bonneuil and Fressoz explain, 'The grand narrative of the Anthropocene is thus a story of an awakening. There was a long moment of unawareness, from 1750 to the late twentieth century, followed by a sudden arousal' (73). But this is not true: 'Far from a narrative of blindness followed by awakening, we thus have a history of the marginalization of knowledge and alerts …. Our planet's entry into the Anthropocene did not follow a frenetic modernism ignorant of the environment but, on the contrary, decades of reflection and concern as to the human degradation of our Earth' (76). In *The Shock of the Anthropocene*, Bonneuil and Fressoz 'explore the existence, since the eighteenth century, of an "environmentalism of the poor" fighting for social justice and environmental decency' (253). We find this in resistance to colonial exploitation, to the enclosure movement, to lose of access to the countryside, and to land and rivers polluted by industrialism. In these, and many other ways, the planet was commodified, and commodification was resisted by those who directly experienced the degradation. But 'The grand narrative of the Anthropocene places *anthropos*, humanity, into two categories: on the one hand, the uninformed mass of the world population, who have become a geological agent without realizing it, and on the other, a small elite of scientists who reveal the dramatic and uncertain future of the planet. In the former, we have a non-reflexive group objectified by demography, biology and economics; in the latter, an idealist history made up of intellectual filiations, precursors and stubborn resistances' (79). In other words, the real resistance to environmental destruction is hidden from view in the grand narrative of the Anthropocene. We see scientists but we never see indigenous peoples struggling against the fossil fuel industry or campaigners putting their liberty at risk to block unnecessary but very profitable developments. When knowledge and the pursuit of profit clash, it is very rare for knowledge to win. Our entry into the Anthropocene was not an accident unnoticed by the many, but 'a political defeat in the face of the forces of free-market economics' (258). As the *Salvage Collective* argue, the concept of the Anthropocene represents a kind of 'political evasion, diluting as it does the necessary focus on capital accumulation' (2021: 15). After the financial crash of 2008, we were all told it was a collective failure, which had to be carried by all. The idea of the Anthropocene makes much the same claim.

We are all asked to share the blame without ever being invited to share the gain. Profits are individualized, while negative consequences are socialized. But we should not lose sight of the brutal equation that the least responsible for the climate crisis are the most vulnerable to its impact. The poorest 10 per cent of the global population produce about 1 per cent of anthropogenic greenhouse gas emissions, whereas the richest 10 per cent are responsible for about 50 per cent (Watson, 2019: 343). Therefore, we should reject the misleading universalism of the Anthropocene. Blaming those without power protects those with power. The ideological advantage of saying it is the personal responsibility of 'the consumer' is that it means governments and corporations can carry on as before.

THE CAPITALOCENE

Many would argue that the Capitalocene is a more accurate term to describe what has happened to the planet. According to Moore, 'the Anthropocene argument poses questions that it cannot answer. The Anthropocene sounds the alarm – and what an alarm it is! But it cannot explain how these alarming changes came about' (2016a: 5). Justin McBrien argues that the Anthropocene 'reinforces what capital wants to believe of itself: that human "nature", not capital, has precipitated today's planetary instability' (2016: 119). But, as Bonneuil and Fressoz point out, 'ninety corporations are responsible for 63 per cent of the cumulative emissions of carbon dioxide and methane between 1850 and today' (2017: 68). In terms of CO_2 emissions, two major capitalist powers dominate:

> Great Britain and the United States made up 60 per cent of cumulative total emissions to date in 1900, 57 per cent in 1950 and almost 50 per cent in 1980 .... The overwhelming share of responsibility for climate change of the two hegemonic powers of the nineteenth (Great Britain) and twentieth (United States) centuries attests to the fundamental link between climate change and projects of world domination .... The entry into the Anthropocene was intrinsically bound up with capitalism .... The history of capitalist world-economies lies at the heart of the changes in the Earth's geological regime, with their Soviet and Chinese avatars being simply a part of this. (116, 117)

To blame us all is apolitical and ahistorical. What defines the new situation is not an age of humans, but the age of capital. Moreover, how we understand a problem helpss shape what we think is the solution. Seeing the climate emergency as something for which we are all equally culpable allows capitalism to present itself not as the problem but as the solution. In other words, the Anthropocene represents a victory of capitalism (including state capitalism) over other possible economic systems. It is not simply that it caused it; rather, what it caused is the inevitable result of its victory.

We are in a situation in which an economic system is at war with the planetary system. Are we in a position to take sides in this conflict? Put simply, if we wish to survive, we have no choice but to side with the planetary system. If we do not, our world, including capitalism, will come to an end. As Klein explains, 'What the climate needs to avoid collapse is a contraction in humanity's use of resources; what our economic model demands to avoid collapse is unfettered expansion. Only one of these sets of rules can be changed, and it's not the laws of nature' (2015: 21). In other words, for our world to survive, capitalism must be changed. We need economic arrangements guided by the principle of health for the many instead of wealth for the few. Capitalism is a system run by the few to serve the interests of the few. Its main supporting argument is that greed is what produces progress. Massive inequalities of wealth are, so the story goes, just temporary, as eventually wealth will 'trickle down' to all of us. In the realm of market fundamentalism, profits are always good, taxes are always bad, corporate regulation is unnecessary, and high wages for the majority and public spending for common services get in the way of economic growth. Capitalism has always put profit before people and before the planet. It is a system which has produced a world in which poverty and plenty are seen as natural companions, and where it seems perfectly acceptable to cut desperately needed benefits to the poor to enable the rich to pay less taxes. An economic culture which does not find such things unconscionable is hardly likely to hesitate when it comes to plundering and polluting the planet.

Moreover, according to Moore (2016b), it is capitalism and not industrialism that has produced the negative impact on the planet.

Therefore, it is important not to conflate capitalism with the Industrial Revolution. The age of capital begins much earlier. As Bonneuil and Fressoz argue,

> to begin the Anthropocene around 1800 obscures the essential fact that industrial capitalism was intensely prepared for by the 'mercantile capitalism' that begun in the sixteenth century, not least in its destructive relationship to nature. To speak of a 'Capitalocene' signals that the Anthropocene did not arise fully armed from the brain of James Watt, the steam engine and coal, but rather from a long historical process of economic exploitation of human beings and the world, going back to the sixteenth century and making industrialism possible.
>
> (2017: 228–229)

Focusing on the Industrial Revolution has 'obscured something hidden in plain sight: the remarkable remaking of land and labor beginning in the long sixteenth century, ca. 1450-1640' (Moore, 2016b: 94). As Moore explains, 'the rise of capitalism after 1450 marked an epochal shift in the scale, speed, and scope of landscape transformation across the geographical expanse of early capitalism' (96). What he calls, 'a new pattern of environment-making' (97). The enclosing of common land in Europe is an obvious example of this new pattern. As Thomas Munster wrote in 1524, 'all creatures have been made into property, the fish in the water, the birds in the air, the plants on the earth' (quoted in Marx, 1992: 239). Much the same point is made a few years earlier in Thomas More's *Utopia* (1516), a text Marx quotes extensively in volume one of *Capital* (Marx, 1976a). As *Utopia's* main character Hythloday explains, 'When I consider and turn over in my mind the various commonwealths flourishing today, so help me God, I can see in them nothing but a conspiracy of the rich, who are advancing their own interests under the name and title of the commonwealth' (More, 2002: 105).

If it begins with the Industrial Revolution, the solution is the end of a certain type of work. However, if it starts with the emergence of capitalism, then the solution required is much more radical. As Moore explains,

To locate the origins of the modern world with the rise of capitalism after 1450, with the audacious strategies of global conquest, endless commodification, and relentless rationalization, is to prioritize a much different politics – one that pursues the fundamental transformation of the relations of power, knowledge, and capital that made the modern world. Shut down a coal plant, and you can slow global warming for a day; shut down the relations that made the coal plant, and you can stop it for good.

(2016b: 94)

We seem trapped in the pages of a story written by capitalism, too often thinking that this is the only possible narrative, the only identity we can ever assume. Green capitalism is a promise that seems unlikely to be fulfilled. Capitalism is a system that must expand or perish. But its relentless pursuit of profit, in which plunder and pollution are always someone else's problem, puts it on a collision course with the planet's finite resources. The excrementitious nonsense of infinite growth on a finite planet is a policy that becomes sovereign everywhere once capitalism is dominant. When the pursuit of ever-increasing growth meets finite resources, the outcome is not difficult to predict. Put simply, capitalism is the problem, not the solution. If our focus is on personal consumption and away from plundering and polluting for profit, we will never get to the heart of the problem. This does not mean that individual decisions are unimportant. By making changes, we can encourage others to change too. But without fundamental change at the level of government and business, our personal changes may achieve very little. However, by acting together, we can make government and business make this more fundamental change, and by saving the planet, we can save ourselves.

NOTES

1 https://commonslibrary.parliament.uk/research-briefings/cbp-8585/ – accessed 7/5/21.

2 What is consumed in rich countries is often produced in poorer parts of the world. Our carbon emissions are thus located elsewhere. Our consumption produces their carbon emissions. While our emissions decline,

those of poorer nations increase. Responsibility for climate change is thus placed with those who produce for our consumption.

3   The fossil fuel industry has funded various so-called think tanks, the main purpose of which is to attack climate science and deny that climate change is something humanly produced. Heavy funding of such foundations is an investment in protecting profits. According to *The Guardian*, between 2002 and 2010, a group of US billionaires, who chose to remain anonymous, donated almost $120 million to 'groups casting doubt about the science behind climate change' (quoted in Klein, 2015: 45).

4   Although Frank Trentmann (2017) dates the origins of consumerism to the fifteenth century in China and India, the primary focus of his research is on the seventeenth century onwards.

5   Like most popular pleasures, especially those practised by women, shopping soon attracted its critics. For example, a man writing in The New York Times (June 1881) complained about 'the awful prevalence of the vice of shopping among women ... [an addiction] every bit as bad as male drinking or smoking' (quoted in Laermans, 1993: 88).

6   See Foucault (1991), especially, 'We must cease once for all to describe the effects of power in negative terms: it "excludes", it "represses", it "censors", it "abstracts", it "masks", it "conceals". In fact, power produces; it produces reality; it produces domains of objects and rituals of truth' (194).

7   Think of the enormous growth in the advertising of gambling on sport and how it presents betting as having little to do with winning and losing money but as itself a sporting activity that gains you self-respect, the esteem of friends, and a social life worth living. This is particularly clear in its redefinition of football, not a game to be played or watched, but as an opportunity to gamble, as if this is the very essence of any match.

8   According to Mark Bould (2021: 143), the term was used informally by Soviet scientists in the 1960s and US scientists in the 1970s.

MEDIATIZED CONSUMPTION

In this chapter, I examine what I am calling mediatized consumption. Mediatization is a concept developed and used in Media Studies and Communications Theory to analyse and describe the increasingly media-saturated world of the twenty-first century. I first explain the concept and then use it to critically explore the everyday experience of being in love and how this has become more and more entangled with the consumption of a variety of media.[1]

MEDIATIZATION

There can be little doubt that media (both discourses and technologies) have in recent years become a very visible feature of everyday life. It is not difficult to see that the world around us has become more and more filled with media. Mediatization is, first, a term used to describe this change. For example, it is now impossible to walk down the high street of any town or city and not see people using mobile phones to talk, text, or take photographs. Similarly, it is hard to imagine a conversation that did not include talk about what is on television or radio, what is showing at the cinema, or what computer game everyone is playing. But mediatization is more than a description of a new phase in the relationship between people and media consumption; it is an attempt to explain this new relationship; an attempt to critically understand the increasing presence and influence of media in social practices of everyday life.

DOI: 10.4324/9781003224471-5

Traditionally, the relationship between media and people has been understood in two quite distinct ways. The first is what has come to be known as the 'media effects' model. Put simply, this sees the media's power in terms of what it does to people. This might be in terms of the politics of news coverage, the morality of Hollywood films, or the persuasive power of advertising. According to this understanding, media cause groups or individuals to change their behaviour: they vote in a new way, their sexual attitudes are modified, or they buy different products. The second understanding, sometimes misleadingly called the 'active audience' model, is focused on consumer activity and points to what people do with media as they use it in their actions and interactions. In other words, instead of media making us do things, according to this model, the interesting question is what we do with media. That is, people act and interact, and during these actions, they use media.

Without denying the significance and importance of these two ways of understanding, mediatization suggests a very different kind of relationship between media and people. When media is understood as either producing effects or being used in social action and interaction, it is always seen as independent of our consumption of it; that is, it is either an outside variable that influences our behaviour or it is a technology we introduce from outside with which we do things. For example, I watch an advert on television and I immediately go out and buy the product advertised. In another scenario, my wife and I watch the same advert together and we use it to remember when we lived in Germany. In this scenario, rather than a mechanism to prompt me to buy something, it becomes the basis for me to remember something. Mediatization suggests that media are more fundamental to our actions and interactions than these approaches, and the two scenarios, I have outlined, seem to suggest. According to mediatization, media are increasingly part of the very fabric of everyday life; it is almost unthinkable without media. But this does not mean that media determines or controls what we do – this is not or should not be another version of technological determinism. Rather, what is being suggested is that media are now fundamental to how we live and how we act and interact with each other.

Mediatization, therefore, represents a new stage in the relationship between media and people. Put simply, media are no longer independent of those they influence or of those who make use of them. Instead, under conditions of mediatization, media are now increasingly entangled in almost all aspects of our lives, not, to repeat the crucial point, as an independent factor but as an integral part of how our lives are increasingly lived. That is, everyday life is no longer simply a place that media influence or where media are used, it is where the acts and interactions of people are now almost unthinkable without media. For example, media have entered the ways of working of many institutions: texting, email, and various forms of online conferencing are now standard tools of business communication. At the same time, media have assumed a greater role as a public arena for news and debate: to such an extent that if it is not in the media, it seems it cannot really be news. This should not be confused with mediation, that is, the use of media to communicate. Although mediatization clearly includes the use of media to communicate, it goes beyond this in that it identifies not just media use but how media use is changing what is communicated and how it is consumed.

Text, email, and various forms of online conferencing are not just a means to communicate; they have changed how we communicate. This does not mean that the media do not produce effects or that people do not use the media in particular ways, but it does mean that media are now in a different relationship with people and have a different place and position in everyday life. For example, the operation of party politics increasingly works through media and is more and more shaped by their logic. By media logic, I do not intend the claim that media operate with a single logic underpinning all their operations, rather I mean that different media in different contexts are increasingly able to shape how non-media institutions act and interact in ways that seem to follow particular media logics. But there is no media logic if by this term we mean the media all operate as one – a Media Industry. However, there is media logic if we think of the different media working in different contexts and helping to shape action and interaction in very particular ways. After all, interaction between media and human agents is crucial – media cannot do it on their own. It is not that media simply influences party politics, as in the media effects model, nor that party politics involves the active use of media, as in the active audience model; rather, it is that media are now a fundamental part of party politics – because of the interweaving between the two, it is now almost impossible to do party politics without media. There can be no doubt that party politics now organizes itself to fit the rhythms of media and that almost all significant political debate is shaped by media. In these ways, media can no longer be seen as outside politics producing media effects or being used in particular ways to mediate politics; they are now fundamental to the very practice of politics. So much so that it is hard to imagine party politics without media. The development in the USA in the 1980s of the 'sound bite', the short phrase or sentence produced explicitly for use on television and radio, and intended to capture the essence of a larger, more complex statement or policy, is an obvious early example of the entanglement of media and party politics.[2] The party leader debates that take place before elections in the UK and USA are another example. These debates are not an example of media effects nor of politicians simply using the media, they are a clear example of the increasing mediatization of party politics – a type of politics that would not exist but for the existence of the media, and which have a significant effect on political outcomes.

MEDIA LOVE

To really understand how mediatization has impacted on consumption is not really a theoretical question, it is more an empirical one; that is, hypothetical speculation must always be supported by grounded ethnographic research. With this in mind, the rest of the chapter will discuss the mediatization of romantic love. The empirical evidence I will draw on to present this case comes from a project called *Media Love*.[3] The aim of the project was to understand the relationship between media and being in love. To be clear, by media love, I do not mean social practices dictated by the media nor do I mean romantic love as represented in the media. Although I discuss how people consume media as part of the architecture and choreography of a romantic relationship, my critical focus is specifically on how media is becoming all the time more fundamental to such relationships. Again, to be clear, the mediatization of romantic love should not be confused with its mediation. It is not just that we increasingly communicate romantically via media (we have been doing this in ever greater numbers since at least the late eighteenth century), rather, it is that media is now transforming our romantic communication. In other words, as both source and medium of romance, media has an increasingly transformative effect on romantic relations.

When we fall in love, we connect to the other person in multiple ways. Many of these connections involve media. We go to the cinema together or we watch television, listen to music or play a computer game; we increasingly have photographs in common; we compare (consciously and unconsciously) our relationship with those we know in literature, film, radio, and television; and when we are not together, we use various media technologies to close down the space between us.

This use of media allows our connection to intensify, and it is this intensification that in part allows ourselves and others to recognize that we are in love. Although I call this media love, I certainly do not think that media have successfully colonized contemporary practices of romantic love. Many aspects of a romantic relationship do not involve consumption of media. Nonetheless, the research shows that contemporary romantic practice has become entangled in, and almost unthinkable without, the consumption of media. There can be little doubt that people increasingly, and actively, consume media as an indispensable part of the production and reproduction of a romantic relationship.

The aim of the research was to explore media–entangled practices of romantic love. I sought to do this without reverting to either media determinism or to the view that romantic love is a simple fact of nature, which people articulate in various ways in moments of emotional and sexual intimacy. Stepping between these two temptations, I tried to show how people consume media to actively make romantic love. I share with actor-network-theory, what it shares with ethnomethodology and practice theory (see discussion in Chapter 6), the view that our everyday social worlds, including practices of romantic love, are not a given, they must be assembled and reassembled. Therefore, I treat media and the consumption of media as existing in networks that materially produce romantic love. Moreover, the consumption of media is not a supplement to contemporary practices of romantic love; it is increasingly fundamental and foundational to the construction and maintenance of such relationships. As Bruno Latour might say, media are intimate actors in these relationships.

The relationship between romantic love and what is sometimes called mass media is historically speaking quite new. Although it is not difficult to find examples of stories of romantic love throughout recorded history, poetry, drama, and mythology being the obvious places to find these, it is only at the end of the eighteenth century, and expanding rapidly throughout the nineteenth and twentieth, that romantic love becomes an increasingly visible part of a shared public culture and a widely accepted means to emotional happiness and sexual fulfilment. As historian Edward Shorter points out, 'The romantic revolution ... began late in the eighteenth century, sweeping across vast reaches of class and territory in the nineteenth to become, in the twentieth, the unassailable norm of courtship behaviour' (1977: 152).

The widespread development of this 'unassailable norm', as something socially visible and widely accepted, and as the main social practice of sexual and emotional intimacy in everyday life, coincided with the development of romantic media. As the historian Lawrence Stone observes, 'after 1780 romantic love and the romantic novel grew together' (1977: 190). The sociologist Anthony Giddens makes much the same point, 'The rise of romantic love more or less coincided with the emergence of the [romantic] novel' (1992: 40).[4] This was also a view shared by contemporary commentators, 'Of all the arrows which Cupid has shot at youthful hearts, [the romantic novel] is the keenest. There is no resisting it. It is literary opium that lulls every sense into delicious rapture' (*The Universal Magazine*, 1772; quoted in Stone, 1977: 190). Moreover, as Francois de la Rochefoucauld claimed, writing a little earlier, 'There are some people who would never have fallen in love if they had not heard there was such a thing' (ibid.: 191). This may have been intended as a mocking jibe at those supposedly too stupid to be able to think for themselves, or to be unable to act without first being told how to act, but I do not think that what he identifies implies stupidity and self-deception; rather I take it as an unknowing recognition of the fact that we actively learn to do many of the things we simply assume to be natural (see Chapter 6). But the real problem with presenting this narrative of the relationship between the consumption of media and romantic love is that it can often imply a one-way flow of influence from media to romantic practice. This is almost certainly what *The Universal Magazine* had in mind when it used the term 'literary opium'. Working from this assumption, the only valid reason to research the relationship between the consumption of media and romantic love is to explore 'media effects' or identify a particular 'media logic'. I totally reject this reduction. Instead, my critical focus includes what people do with media, rather than simply what media make them do.[5] This does not mean a denial of media influence, but a recognition that influence is not an inevitable consequence of supposed passivity, but a complex process that almost always involves agency and use. But to reiterate, I am trying to suggest something more than mediation of romantic relationships; I am thinking of media as a mediator, as an actor in the romantic relationship (for the distinction between mediators and intermediaries, see the discussion of actor-network-theory in Chapter 6).

What is clear from the findings of the *Media Love* project is that people do not passively consume media and then translate this unproblematically and straightforwardly into social practices of romantic love. Instead, the project continually encountered a dialogue between media and the active consumption practices of people in love. In Storey and McDonald (2013), I argue that the best way to understand the romantic power of media is to conceptualize it as working like a language; a 'language' we must work with in order to communicate our romantic feelings to others and to ourselves. To be clear, I do not mean media literally provide the language of romantic love, although at times they may in fact do this; rather I am suggesting that the discourses media produce work like a language in that they enable and constrain social practices of romantic love (see discussion of discourse in Chapter 1). To be in love, therefore, is to locate oneself in a mediatized network of meanings and practices (often contradictory) produced and/or circulated by media which establish a system of romantic 'common sense' (Gramsci, 1971) or what might be called, to borrow from Foucault, a romantic 'regime of truth' (Foucault, 2002). And because media discourses of romantic love operate like a language, we need to recognize that the performance of a language and language as a system are quite different: the language spoken does not dictate the act of speaking; the speaker actively selects from the resources the language makes available. In this way, then, although media discourses of romantic love both enable and constrain agency, they certainly do not dictate romantic practice as would be assumed by the 'media effects' model. It is like speaking any language, we are situated in a mediatized structure that both enables and constrains our ability to understand and communicate and, as with language competence generally, there are different levels of media-derived romantic literacy. Umberto Eco's much-quoted definition of the postmodern attitude I think points to this. 'I think of the postmodern attitude as that of a man who loves a very cultivated woman and knows he cannot say to her "I love you madly", because he knows that she knows (and she knows that he knows) that these words have already been written by Barbara Cartland' (1985: 17). This may or may not identify a postmodern attitude, but for me, it certainly identifies people with high levels of media-derived romantic literacy. Media, therefore, do not directly shape romantic practice, rather they provide the language from which romantic practice is articulated – a mediatized structure that both enables and constrains romantic agency. But and this is a very important but, we must stay within the 'common sense' of the romantic 'regime of truth' in order to remain romantically intelligible to others and to ourselves. As a result, romantic practice (even in all its contradictory variety) only becomes recognizable as romantic practice through conformity with media-derived standards of romantic intelligibility (to deviate from these standards may cause 'translation' problems). This does not mean that our experiences of being in love are a form of pre-scripted 'false consciousness' in which our emotional reactions are simple media creations. What the *Media Love* interviewees[6] made clear is that media do not have the effect of dictating romantic practice. Instead, they offer a language, and like any language, it allows people to use it to articulate the meaning of their own experiences of romantic love. Part of the form this agency takes is in the way media discourses are both recognized and negotiated with (see Storey and McDonald, 2013).

Listening romantically to music is a good example of the active consumption of media. As expected, many of the interviewees talked about how particular songs had played a significant role in their romantic experiences. Although many of the interviewees identified music as something to relax with or as a background to a romantic setting, most suggested that music was almost always used to reactivate a romantic memory; it had an archival function in that it allowed them to return affectively to a romantic situation in the past. Interviewee 6 gave a typical response. 'It's not something that particularly enhances it for me as in when I'm falling in love or if I am in love. I don't think the music is something I think about at the time. For me it has always been afterwards'. Interviewee 4 made a similar point. 'It was playing when I first got together with somebody in a relationship, and I always remember that song'. Interviewee 2 talked of how it 'reminded me …. I'm not going to regret it; it does remind me'. Interviewee 1 remarked that 'every time I hear that song it always reminds me of that incident'. He also explained about how other songs always made him think of her. It was very clear that these songs had a powerful affective charge in their ability to enable him to rearticulate the past. 'I think of her straightaway …. Sometimes it can be a bit sad. You know like, I think it depends on what mood you're in, cos sometimes when I hear that song I think, oh, yeah that was a really good night, we had a really good time. Then other times I think, oh, I'm never gonna be with her'. Interviewee 6 used music in much the same way.

> I think with music and the emotion of love, I think sometimes when you have been in love and you hear music, you do especially if you're on your own, you relate things that are in that music to yourself …. Lately, over the last four or five weeks, since I decided to distance myself from the girl I was telling you about I was in a bit of a situation. I would say I was probably in a bit of a vulnerable state of mind, and I was listening to music. Sometimes, if it was on and I would find it was actually making me more kind of sad and making me think of that person more.

What is clear is that each interviewee consumes music in different ways to remember. But what is also the case is that their consumption of music is fundamental to the act of remembering – music and memory are entangled together to such an extent that I wonder if these memories would really exist without the music. There is a song by Eric Church in which he sings 'Funny how a melody sounds like a memory'.[7] It is this transformation of melody into memory – the mediatization of romantic memory – to which each of the interviewees is drawing attention.

The two most important technologies identified by the interviewees when being or falling in love were texting and Facebook. Texting was the media technology mentioned the most. Interviewee 9 gave a typical response: 'I'd say 90 percent of the communication is by text and then I'd say mobile phone for like a quick ten min phone call here and there'. Sometimes the romantic relationship itself seemed to be held together by acts of texting. For example, Interviewee 6 speaks of a relationship that was almost entirely based on texting,

> We just got on really well and we saw each other about three or four times I think over about six weeks …. [A]nd then we were texting a lot. A lot of it was based on texts and sending messages to each other and the fact that we only saw each other four times out of those six weeks I suppose was kind of irrelevant in the sense because we were texting a lot.

Many interviewees were very clear that texting had the effect of accelerating the development of their romantic relationship. 'I think it speeds things up more than anything, because now with phones [for texting] you can constantly be in contact' (Interviewee 10). Interviewee 9 made much the same point. 'I think I'm closer to her because you get to know someone quicker cos you're texting them and like we do text quite a bit. And like in the early stages of us getting together *that's kind of like how we got to know each other* and like we were texting quite a bit and so I think it does help you get to know them a bit closer' (my italics). Again, this is not simple mediation; it is mediatization. Often it was the extent of texting that produced this quickening effect. 'Constantly, it wouldn't stop, it was ridiculous, our phones would be silent if we were together. But if we weren't together then they would be constantly going off. Even if we'd only been together that hour and I'd just come into uni for an hour he'd be texting me making sure I was OK, even though I'd be going back to his after …. It was constant. The only reason we would stop is if I was in a lecture or he was in an exam at college' (Interviewee 8). In these examples, particularly the last one, texting is not simply a means to communicate romantic feelings; it is a fundamental part of the actual fabric of the relationship.

Part of the speeding up was in terms of sexual intimacy. 'I think you can be a bit more risky, a bit more rude, a bit more cheeky' (Interviewee 1). 'I think it's easier for people to let themselves get more intimate than what it previously would've been' (Interviewee 10). 'Yeah, I think especially when you're getting to know them, it's easier to be a bit more brash than say if you just met them on the street out of the blue. I don't think you'd be like, huh [he makes a noise suggesting sexual excitement]' (Interviewee 9). Interviewee 8 pointed out how, in this context, texting could provide a screen to hide behind; a mechanism to enable things to be said that, if necessary, could be disavowed. 'Yeah, you've got more confidence to message each other haven't you. Rather than face to face .... I think in a message you can hide behind the words a bit: oh, I didn't mean to send you that .... I was drunk. If you say something stupid, my friend sent it. You've got a million excuses to not mean what you wanted to say'. It is very clear that for Interviewee 8 the ability to be able to deny or disown an intended meaning ('a million excuses to not mean what you wanted to say') is very liberating. Interviewee 6 also found texting gave him a similar kind of freedom.

> I try to act the same in texts as I would do in person, but then I think that you do find yourself talking on text, or in fact on Facebook chat, you find yourself saying things that you probably truly wouldn't say in person .... [W]hen you're looking somebody in the eye, I think it's sometimes difficult to actually say what you want to say.

According to Interviewee 13, texting 'helped us seduce each other .... It allowed us to express ourselves and say those things which made us feel the urge and need for the other person even more .... It was precisely through text messages ... that very "romantic" and breath-taking things were said between us'. Interviewee 11 gave an example that went well beyond the speeding up of sexual intimacy. In her case, texting was in fact a form of sexual intimacy.

My last relationship ... began with a (tipsy) text message after not having seen each other in five years, and then largely developed by texting, email, and Skype (without video) before we were able to see each other [at the time they were living in different countries]. So, in that case, the falling in love part really happened without any face-to-face interaction.

When they eventually met, their technologically enabled sex life continued into their face-to-face relationship, but in ways she found slightly estranging. As she explained,

I also felt that this [their previous text life] influenced how the relationship then actually worked. I remember, for instance, coming to [she names the place where her boyfriend lived] after months of not having seen each other, and what alienated me was that he immediately verbalised [as in a text] what he wanted to do when I had barely entered the house. Somehow, having just kissed me passionately and then went on to do what he was talking about would have been different [and by implication far more satisfying].

Sometimes the speeding up caused by texting can have other negative effects. As Interviewee 10 explained, 'But with texting it happens in fast motion, um, um, really fast, because I had a relationship with someone where we went out for a month and I really liked them, but from texting each other it just went down hill from there'. She identified the major reason for this negative effect: 'I think cos it's always in contact quite a lot ... there's not really a lot to say when you've met up afterwards'. In other words, in her experience, constant texting can reveal too much too soon or it can simply feel like a prison house of too much knowledge and expectation. Interviewee 2 complained that constant texting denied him space. 'I wanted space and she wouldn't give it to me, so I just left my phone at home every now and then'. It later became clear in the interview that leaving his phone at home meant telling her he had left it at home.

Texting can create other difficulties in a romantic relationship. Interviewee 14, who described her younger self as a 'love detective', always on the look out for evidence of attraction, had a very different experience of the possible problems associated with texting, one that nevertheless indicates how important it is as a measure of romantic attachment and seriousness. 'I had the misfortune to fall in love with a very unenthusiastic texter … which meant that a low response rate to text was interpreted as evidence of a lack of interest'. It seems that too much or too little texting can undermine the foundations of a romantic relationship, a relationship that texting itself had helped to establish.

Text messaging also has the potential to create and maintain a quite detailed record of the romantic relationship. It can work like an electronic diary, but, unlike a conventional diary, one in which are stored comments from both sides of the relationship. As Interviewee 6 explains,

> I think looking back, cos that's one thing you will do with text messages, cos your mobile phone will store a lot of messages …. I think when you have a situation like this [he is referring to the end of a romantic relationship] one of the things you find yourself doing, which is probably more harmful than helpful, is looking back on everything you have said, and I did that and it was actually quite interesting. I don't think it was harmful for me because it was more interesting to see what had happened …. It was interesting to try and find out why this individual had made me act differently and had made me feel differently, and how come it upset me and made me generally unhappy when things weren't working.

Many of the interviewees included Facebook when talking about texting. They tended to use it in similar ways and, like texting, thought of it in relation to romantic relationships in both positive and negative terms. Interviewee 3, whose boyfriend was overseas, talked about 'romantic times when we used to instant message each other on Facebook'. When asked what they talked about, she replied, 'The boring things, like what I had done during the day and stuff …. I think it's really important to have that sort of contact when someone is away for that long'. It is clear that Facebook allowed them to maintain their romantic relationship in circumstances that put the relationship under great strain. So, it was not just a means of communication (mediation); it was a fundamental part of their mediatized relationship. Like Interviewee 3, Interviewee 7 explained that much of the conversation she has with her boyfriend on Facebook is often quite mundane. In addition to this, they would also do other things while they chatted. 'I will be doing essays and that when I'm talking to him and I'll say, oh, I'm not in the mood to do this essay and he says, yes, but if you just get it done it's out of the way. If he's had a really bad day at work, I'll say, oh, it'll be fine, it's just another day at work. If I'm watching TV, I'll tell him about it, and he'll tell me about the [computer] game he's playing and things like that'. Clearly, Facebook allows them to talk and develop their relationship in a way that would normally only be possible in a situation of co-presence. Again, this is not mediation; it is mediatization. Interviewee 11 used Skype in ways similar to how Interviewees 3 and 7 used Facebook.

> [We would] Skype very often all day when we are both at home. We then usually go about our own business most of the time but feel that the other is there …. We both work … but I have the iPad next to me and can glance at him every once in a while; or we leave it on when we go to sleep, and I might sleep already but he is still reading, or we have breaks together or in the end spend the evening together as if we had a proper date.

She then added,

> I think that especially in times like these, when everyone is expected to be flexible and mobile in career terms, these media make a huge difference in how close you can feel to each other in spite of the distance, and it can enable at least a variety of everyday life together.

Like texting, Facebook also has the potential to undermine what it has helped to develop and establish. As Interviewee 3 explained, 'you can see on Facebook their ex and their ex emailing them cos they still got a house together that they can't get rid of. I think that makes that relationship a bit more complicated'. She described another complication when she discovered photographs of her boyfriend's ex-girlfriend in his Facebook album. As she pointed out, 'she wasn't wearing that much clothes and obviously they upset me'. It became clear that it wasn't just that these photographs existed, but that they existed in a public space available for friends and family to see: 'if it was printed photos, I kind of understand that he would have photos of his ex around cos they were together quite a while'. So, the photographs themselves were not the problem, it was their public location that really caused her to feel disappointed and upset. 'I also felt a little humiliated, cos it's on Facebook so everyone can see that he has still got pictures of his ex, which kind of reflects on me'. Interviewee 5 was also aware of the problem of photographs, and information more generally, being available on Facebook.

> If there is any pictures of me with like ex-girlfriends or girls I used to see [an interesting distinction], when I break up with them, I remove them, cos the last thing you want to do when you're looking at someone's Facebook and saying, oh, that's what their ex looks like … [I]f she meets a lad, he's gonna be like, wow, look at all these things, her and the ex-boyfriend … and that's gonna put him under pressure … and he's like shit, he bought her this hotel [a couple of nights in a hotel], they went to London for the weekend. I'm broke, what do I do? If there was no social network and then that lad would know nothing about me, he wouldn't be able to click on profile to see where I'm from or what I do or whatever. He would probably forget about my name after a week.

Without Facebook, the situation identified by Interviewees 3 and 5 would not be possible. Again, the technology does not mediate the relationship; it is part of its mediatized structure.

Interviewee 5 pointed to the ways texting and Facebook are changing the practical possibilities of romance. 'Thirty years ago, when my Dad met Mum, he said when he met her the next day he would phone her. See if you done that now the girl might go, here, I don't remember you. By texts or Facebook, they don't have to reply and if they don't reply you know they are not interested'. Interviewee 6 gave another example of how Facebook is changing romantic practice. 'If you see somebody on a night out and you get talking to them they would probably find it less personally invading to be asked if they could be your friend on Facebook than to ask for their number'. But this simple switch from one technology to another may not be as benign as it sounds; it can lead to what he calls 'Facebook stalking'.

> If I know nothing about her, I go on their Facebook and I can find out every single thing about her; I can look through her pictures and see what her ex-boyfriend looked like, what her friends are like, what she likes .... Like, 'I like a man who holds my hand in the dark', say. You can tell everything they like and that's really scary because when you go on the first date you know everything about them and you're asking them questions that you already know [the answers]. You're asking them what do you study and it's written on the top of her Facebook.

Consequently, a first date may seem 'traditional', but it could be prepared for and structured by information that would have been unthinkable to lovers in the past; that is, inconceivable to lovers before the mediatization of romantic love.

PRELIMINARY CONCLUSIONS

The concern of the *Media Love* project was with how people consume media. So, I did not begin with media and then examine their use; rather, I began with accounts of everyday experiences of romantic love and then attempted to tease out how these were enabled and constrained by media consumption. During the interviews, there was no attempt made to define romantic love or how we might define what counts as media. In each interview, it was the interviewee who decided what these terms describe and delimit. The focus of the project, therefore, was not on the media of romantic love, but on how people consume media to make romantic love, to make it socially manifest in practice. Therefore, while it is true that texting and Facebook enable a new kind of romantic communication and constrain the form this communication may take, they do not determine that we communicate, nor what we communicate, this is always a matter of agency and use. However, what is also clear is that the two traditional models I discussed at the beginning of this chapter, media effects and active audience, cannot adequately explain the relationship between the consumption of media and practices of romantic love. Instead, what the interviews show is a more intense, complex, and contradictory relationship, one I think that is best captured by the concept of mediatized consumption.

NOTES

1 For a detailed discussion of mediatization, see Hepp (2013) and Hjarvard (2013).

2 One of the earliest, and perhaps most famous, sound bites can be found in a speech made by President Ronald Reagan in Berlin in June 1987. Referring to the Berlin Wall, the speech includes the phrase, 'Mr. Gorbachev, tear down this wall'. Although the sentence is part of a longer speech, it seems clear that this was intended to be extracted for media consumption. British Prime Minister Boris Johnson, a specialist in politics as consumption, has made a political career of using such sound bites, hoping, with some success, that voters will rest satisfied with the rhetoric and fail to act or even see the reality that is being masked.

3 For details of the Media Love project, see Storey and McDonald (2013).

4 Interestingly, the rise of romantic love also more or less coincided with the emergence of capitalist consumer society (see discussion in Chapters 2 and 4 here).

5 Marx also uses the metaphor of opium in his famous description of religion as 'the opium of the people' (1992: 244). But unlike *The Universal Magazine*, he does not see it as a simple question of influence. Less famously, Marx also says of religion that it is 'the expression of real suffering and a protest against suffering' (ibid.). In other words, again unlike *The Universal Magazine*, his metaphor includes both what people do in concert with what is done to them. Also see discussion of 'compromise equilibrium' (Gramsci) in Chapter 7.

6 Media Love interviewees

> Interviewee 1: male, British, straight, aged 19.
> Interviewee 2: male, British, straight, aged 19.
> Interviewee 3: female, British, straight, aged 25.
> Interviewee 4: male, British, gay, aged 19.
> Interviewee 5: male, British, straight, aged 23.
> Interviewee 6: male, British, straight, aged 21.
> Interviewee 7: female, British, straight, aged 19.
> Interviewee 8: female, British, straight, aged 19.

Interviewee 9: male, British, straight, aged 19.
Interviewee 10: female, British, straight, aged 19.
Interviewee 11: female, German, bisexual, aged 36.
Interviewee 12: female, Austrian, straight, aged 30.
Interviewee 13: female, Spanish, straight, aged 33.
Interviewee 14: female, Irish, straight, aged 34.

7 The song is called 'Springsteen' and is available on *Chief* and *Caught in the Act*. The second album is a live recording in which he talks about the events that inspired the song. Part of what he says seems to capture what Interviewees 2, 4, and 6 experienced: 'I had a melody connect itself with a memory'.

CONSUMPTION AND EVERYDAY LIFE

Consumption is fundamental to the routines and habits of everyday life. This chapter explores how we might understand this relationship. Everyday life has a long and complex history as an object of study in sociology.[1] In this chapter, I critically examine five sociological accounts: symbolic interactionism, ethnomethodology, phenomenological sociology, actor-network-theory, and practice theory. What each of these sociological traditions brings to a conceptualization of everyday life is the valuable insistence that we should always look beyond what appears to exist quite naturally to how it exists socially and in so doing we should fully recognize its human constructedness. Consumption is fundamental to this process.

SYMBOLIC INTERACTIONISM

Symbolic interactionism began in the work of the 'Chicago School', the University of Chicago's department of sociology. Fundamental to its foundation and development was the study of everyday life. Moreover, from the beginning, there was a determination that such investigations must be 'naturalistic'. By naturalistic, they meant the insistence that it must be studied as it exists in the everyday and not as it might or should exist in theoretical speculations about everyday life in lecture theatre or seminar room. This produced several ground-breaking studies. Perhaps the most significant of these are Frederick Thrasher's *The Delinquent Gang* (1927), Louis Wirth's *The Ghetto* (1928), Harvey Zorbaugh's *The Gold Coast and the Slum* (1929), and Clifford Shaw's *The*

DOI: 10.4324/9781003224471-6

Jack-Roller (1930). However, it was not until the second generation of scholars at Chicago that the term 'symbolic interactionism' was used to name this new sociological methodology. Herbert Blumer, who first coined the term, provides a very clear definition of this sociological way of working. It is worth quoting in full to be able to understand its conceptualization of a new methodology.

> Symbolic interactionism rests in the last instance on three simple premises. The first premise is that human beings act toward things on the basis of the meaning that the things have for them. Such things include everything that the human being may note in his world – physical objects, such as trees or chairs; other human beings, such as a mother or a store clerk; categories of human beings such as friends or enemies; institutions, such as a school or a government; guiding ideals, such as individual independence or honesty; activities of others, such as their commands or requests; and such situations as an individual encounters in his daily life. The second premise is that the meaning of such things is derived from, or arises out of, the social interaction that one has with one's fellows. The third premise is that these meanings are handled in, and modified through, an interpretative process used by the person in dealing with the things he encounters.
>
> (1969: 2)

What is clear is that symbolic interactionism sees consumption as existing in a world of meanings and social actions and interactions. Viewing consumption in this way is a rejection of any perspective that understands it as being the result of conscious or unconscious, genetic or environmental, factors that determine such actions and interactions. These supposed determining forces can take various forms: for example, psychological stimuli, social pressures, genetic disposition, and economic forces. In each instance, either the force causing a social action or the resulting social action excludes human agency; the meaning of the action for the individual is either ignored or subsumed in the act itself. For example, if a young man, walking with friends in a shopping centre, suddenly starts to cry, this might be explained by what caused the crying (he has just received a text telling him that his girlfriend has found a new boyfriend) or the act of crying itself (the release of fluid from the lacrimal gland). In both cases, the meaning of crying in public for the young man and his friends is either ignored or subsumed under cause or act. Contrary to this, symbolic interactionism seeks to investigate what the act of crying means for the individual crying and the society in which he cries. So, what would happen? His friends would interact with him because of the symbolic meaning of his tears. They would 'just know' that standing in a public place with tears rolling down his face is an obvious sign that he is distressed and in need of comfort. They would not rush for a medical knowledge of lacrimation; they would interact with him based on tears as a sign of sadness. During the interaction, they may ask him about the cause of his tears, but the important thing is to first comfort him. Of course, once the interaction deepens, the cause of his tears will itself become an object with meaning. The significant thing here for symbolic interactionism is that the interaction of friends comforting a young man crying in public is a consequence of the meaning of his tears and not the tears themselves or their cause.

This takes us to the second premise about the source of meaning. There is a long tradition of regarding the meaning of something as intrinsic to the thing itself. The meaning of crying, for example, is intrinsic to the act of crying. Meaning is inherent and emanates from the thing in question. Another tradition sees meaning as a personal act of ascription. Crying means this to you and something else to me. Perhaps the most established version of this perspective is Freudianism, where the meaning of a dream, say, can be successfully established only by making use of the dreamer's associations (Freud, 1973; Storey, 2021a). Symbolic interactionism rejects both these versions of the making of meaning. Instead, it insists that meanings are always 'social products'; they are 'creations that are formed in and through the defining activities of people as they interact' (5). In other words, the making of meaning is a collective activity that emerges from social interaction. Moreover, our understanding of the meaning of a situation informs how we act, in that we do not respond to the meaning of a situation as an external factor, rather how we understand it as meaningful is fundamental and inseparable from how we act. Everyday life, therefore, is not a world in which action is either a response to or an embodiment of external forces; it is a process in which interpretation and action are almost inseparable. As Blumer points out, we need to pay attention to 'the vital process of interpretation in which the individual notes and assesses what is presented to him and through which he maps out lines of overt behaviour prior to their execution' (15). It was because his friends shared an understanding of the meaning of a young man crying in public that they knew how to act and interact. If one of the friends buys him a drink to consume, this is because they think this is a natural way to respond. Sitting in a bar talking about it is what one is supposed to do. It is normal; a normality to be accepted and acted upon.

The third premise involves meaning as a process of interpretation. Although meanings are formed during social interaction, they are not 'a mere application of established meanings but ... a formative process in which meanings are used and revised as instruments for the guidance and formation of action' (ibid.). In other words, meanings are not applied in social interaction, as if they came from somewhere else; they are a fundamental part of the interaction itself. We do not engage in action and interaction in everyday life and then introduce meaning; meanings are a constitutive part of the very fabric of social interaction. The meaning of the young man's tears, and the meaning of the acts of comfort from his friends, is inseparable from the social interaction that occurred when he received the text as they walked through the shopping centre. It is inseparable from them all sitting together in the bar drinking.

Based on these three premises, symbolic interactionism sees everyday life as consisting of people engaging in meaningful action. 'The action consists of the multitudinous activities that the individuals perform in their life as they encounter one another and as they deal with the succession of situations confronting them' (6). These actions, both individual and collective, are what define everyday life and how and what we consume is fundamental to this definition. As Blumer puts it, 'society exists in action and must be seen in terms of action ... human society consists of people engaging in action' (6, 7). Most of this action is in fact social interaction, people interacting with one another and what they consume around them. Again, we should not see only the causes or outcomes of this interaction and miss the interaction itself. To repeat, it is the interaction that is fundamental to the workings of everyday life. According to Blumer,

> social interaction is a process that forms human conduct instead of being merely a means or a setting for the expression or release of human conduct. Put simply, human beings in interacting with one another have to take account of what each other is doing or is about to do; they are forced to direct their own conduct or handle their situations in terms of what they take into account. (8)

In other words, what others do and say enables and constrains what we do and say. If I go to work with the intention of doing A and a colleague asks me to do B, I may do B or I may explain why I must do A first. In this way, my intentions are either changed or postponed because of my interaction with my colleague. If something that has happened in my life makes me very happy and I go to lunch with a friend who is very unhappy, it would seem very inappropriate to display my happiness in the presence of my friend's sadness. In both examples, I would consider the actions or intended actions of others, and it is this taking into account that helps shape our social interactions. Again, in the example of the young man crying in the shopping centre, all the interactions that took place were a consequence of considering the actions of others.

Social interaction can take one of two forms: non-symbolic and symbolic. The first is action of a direct kind, a reflex response that does not involve an interpretation of the action of the other. For example, a friend knocks over a bottle of wine and I automatically move to one side to stop the wine from flowing into my lap. However, we rarely respond directly to the action of another, rather our response is usually based on our interpretation of the meaning we attach to the action. So, if my friend was drunk and it was becoming increasingly obvious that she might knock something over and I adjust my position so as to be more able to move quickly if in fact she does do this, then I am engaging in symbolic interaction; I have interpreted the situation and acted accordingly. Both forms of social interaction are to be found in everyday life. As Blumer explains,

In their association human beings engage plentifully in non-symbolic interaction as they respond immediately and unreflectively to each other's bodily movements, expressions, and tones of voice, but their characteristic mode of interaction is on the symbolic level, as they seek to understand the meaning of each other's action. (8–9)

Everyday life consists of the giving and taking of meaning as we interact with others. If someone makes a gesture towards me, and because meaning is not intrinsic, I must interpret the gesture. Part of what I must figure out is if the gesture means the same thing for both of us. If it does, we have understanding. In everyday life, we do not encounter the simple playing out of meanings that pre-exist it, rather it is the giving and taking of meanings in social interaction that produce what we recognize as everyday life. The friends who responded to the young man's tears were not simply following a pre-existing model of interaction, they were interpreting the situation and then acting not just as friends but in a way that produces and reproduces friendship. In other words, their actions were formative. When one of the friends buys the young man a drink to consume, thinking that this is what friends do, in this doing, friendship is produced and reproduced. As Blumer explains,

Human society or group consists of people in association. Such association exists necessarily in the form of people acting toward one another and thus engaging in social interaction. Such interaction in human society is characteristically and predominantly on the symbolic level; as individuals acting individually, collectively, or as agents of some organization encounter one another they are necessarily required to take account of the actions of one another as they form their own action. They do this by a dual process of indicating to others how to act and of interpreting the indications made by others .... By virtue of symbolic interaction, human group life is necessarily a formative process and not a mere arena for the expression of pre-existing factors. (10)

According to Blumer, everyday life is constructed out of the many 'lines of action' (20) that are a consequence of people interacting with each other and with the objects that surround them, including consumption. For symbolic interactionism, we are social in a quite particular way. We are social not only in our interactions with others but also in our interactions with ourselves. Our capacity for self-reflection (seeing oneself as an 'object') allows us to be in dialogue with ourselves and to engage in inner discussions ('self-indications') to organize and carry out our social interactions. But despite all the talk of action and interaction, Blumer also identifies repetition and stability.

> The preponderant portion of social action in a human society, particularly in a settled society, exists in the form of recurrent patterns of joint action. In most situations in which people act toward one another they have in advance a firm understanding of how to act and of how other people will act. They share common and pre-established meanings of what is expected in the action of the participants, and accordingly each participant is able to guide his own behaviour by such meanings. Instances of repetitive and preestablished forms of joint action are so frequent and common that it is easy to understand why scholars have viewed them as the essence or natural form of human group life. (18)

But the apparent repetition of pre-established meanings gives a very misleading picture of the reality of everyday life. With its focus on the supposed passive following of rules, it totally fails to see the action and interaction that sustains everyday life and makes it visible. As Blumer explains, 'It is the social process in group life that creates and upholds the rules, not the rules that create and uphold group life' (19). So, what is this social process? Well, first it is not a self-governing network or system in which humans are simply passive participants. If it is a network or a system, it 'does not function automatically because of some inner dynamics or system requirements; it functions because people at different points do something, and what they do is a result of how they define the situation in which they are called to act' (ibid.).

The world of the everyday is composed of objects. These objects are the product of symbolic interaction. An object can be anything that can be referenced in some way. There are three types of objects: physical, social, and abstract. Physical objects include tables, flowers, and buses. A mother, a friend, or a teacher are counted as social objects. Political positions or religious doctrines, or ideas of equality or romantic love, are regarded as abstract objects. 'The nature of an object – of any and every object - consists of the meaning that it has for the person for whom it is an object.

This meaning sets the way in which he sees the object, the way in which he is prepared to act toward it, and the way in which he is ready to talk about it' (11). Objects may have different meanings for different people. A horse may have a different meaning for a jockey, a trainer, a schoolgirl, a farmer, or an artist. 'The meaning of objects for a person arises fundamentally out of the way they are defined to him by others with whom he interacts' (ibid.). Significant others would include parents, teachers, friends, media, and governments. In the mutual interactions of everyday life, a certain consensus of meaning is achieved. 'Out of a process of mutual indications common objects emerge – objects that have the same meaning for a given set of people and are seen in the same manner' (ibid.). The tears cried in the shopping centre were clearly a shared object for the young man and his friends. It is an example of the consensus of meaning that makes everyday life appear as taken for granted. But it also remains true that everyday life can consist of different 'worlds' in which objects have particular meanings. Youth subcultures would be an obvious example of a different 'world' of meaning. If we are to understand these different worlds, we must identify their objects and the meanings they are made to carry. Moreover, the meaning of an object is always a social creation, it is formed, and it arises out of acts of definition and interpretation that take place in social interaction. According to Blumer, 'social interaction is a formative process in its own right ... people in interaction are not merely giving expression to such determining factors in forming their respective lines of action but are directing, checking, bending, and transforming their lines of action in the light of what they encounter in the actions of others' (53). Based on previous interactions, we develop a common understanding of how to act in a particular situation. Everyday life, therefore, does not surround a person with pre-existing objects that then enable and constrain his or her activity; rather objects are constructed as meaningful in ongoing social interaction.

The meaning of anything and everything has to be formed, learned, and transmitted through a process of indication - a process that is necessarily a social process. Human group life on the level of symbolic interaction is a vast process in which people are forming, sustaining, and transforming the objects of their world as they come to give meaning to objects. Objects have no fixed status except as their meaning is sustained through indications and definitions that people make of their objects. Nothing is more apparent than that objects in all categories can undergo change in their meaning .... In short, from the standpoint of symbolic interactionism human group life is a process in which objects are being created, affirmed, transformed, and cast aside. The life and action of people necessarily change in line with the changes taking place in their world of objects. (12)

Everyday life, according to symbolic interactionism,

is a process of activity in which participants are developing lines of action in the multitudinous situations they encounter. They are caught up in a vast process of interaction in which they have to fit their developing actions to one another. This process of interaction consists in making indications to others of what to do and in interpreting the indications as made by others. They live in worlds of objects and are guided in their orientation and action by the meaning of these objects. Their objects, including objects of themselves, are formed, sustained, weakened, and transformed in their action with one another. (20–21)

The everyday, therefore, is constructed from the social interactions that generate the meanings that sustain its taken-for-grantedness. The friends in the shopping centre, with their actions and interactions, created and sustained a little part of what we think of as everyday life. Similarly, when we consume, our actions and interactions produce and reproduce what we call consumption.

ETHNOMETHODOLOGY

According to Harold Garfinkel, everyday life is 'an ongoing accomplishment of the concerted activities of daily life, with the ordinary, artful ways of that accomplishment being by members known, used, and taken for granted' (1967: vii). Moreover, 'In the actual occasions of interaction that accomplishment is for members omnipresent, unproblematic, and commonplace' (9). Everyday life has 'an accomplished sense, an accomplished facticity, an accomplished objectivity, an accomplished familiarity, an accomplished accountability' (10). But the making of everyday life, its accomplishment, is not something that its makers are ever fully conscious of doing. It is done with little fuss: 'for the member the organizational hows of these accomplishments are unproblematic, are known vaguely, and are known only in the doing which is done skilfully, reliably, uniformly, with enormous standardization and as an unaccountable matter' (ibid.). In other words, to reiterate what we have seen in symbolic interactionism, it is taken for granted. The friends in the shopping centre simply take for granted that what they were doing was the normal thing to do. Similarly, being in a shopping centre on a Saturday afternoon, shopping and not shopping, simply consuming the shopping centre, is something they take for granted.

Everyday life consists of taken-for-granted meanings and expectations that produce routine patterns of social life. So much of this consists of unstated assumptions that constitute the common sense of social action and interaction. If everyday life is, as Garfinkel maintains, 'a contingent accomplishment of socially organized common practices' (33), the point of analysis is to answer 'the general question of how any such common sense world is possible' (36). The task of ethnomethodology is to make 'the commonplace scenes visible', to make evident the 'background expectancies' that act as 'a scheme of interpretation' (ibid.). Put simply, to make the unnoticed become noticed. Why did the friends in the shopping centre think it was normal to act as they did? Why do they think it is normal to spend most of Saturday afternoon in a shopping centre? What kind of consumption are they engaging in? Ethnomethodology seeks to account for this practical accomplishment, to dismantle the accomplishment in order to show that it is an accomplishment and to reveal how and why it works. Or, as Garfinkel himself expresses it, 'I use the term "ethnomethodology" to refer to the investigation of the rational properties of indexical expressions and other practical actions as contingent ongoing accomplishments of organized artful practices of everyday life' (11).

What particularly concerns ethnomethodology, as its name implies, are the methods people employ in their daily activities. These activities produce everyday life – 'an endless, ongoing, contingent accomplishment' (1) – and make it visible to sociological analysis. Everyday life does not produce human activities; it is human activities that produce everyday life. Without these activities, the everyday would not exist. In other words, Garfinkel is not concerned with the social structure of the everyday but with the structuring activities that make the structure visible. But he goes further than this: without these activities, there would be no structure. The social structure of everyday life is something that must be assembled and reassembled by the social activities of its members. The response of the friends to the young man crying did not happen in everyday life; it was part of what we recognize as everyday life. Moreover, what they were in the shopping centre to do assembles and reassembles the practice of shopping (with or without purchase): without shoppers, shopping ceases to exist.

Ethnomethodology starts from the assumption that we all take for granted the background expectancies that make everyday life seem so natural and routine. If, for example, you think of everyday life as working like a conversation between two close friends, to really understand what they are saying, we must pay attention to the gaps and absences that are structuring what is being said – the things that are so obvious as to not need articulating. But for us to really understand what is being said, we must find a way to articulate these gaps and absences. Ethnomethodology uses various strategies to try to articulate these background expectancies. For example, it seeks to disrupt the normal routines of everyday life to understand it as something assembled by human actions. Garfinkel argues that 'to produce disorganized interaction should tell us something about how the structures of everyday activities are ordinarily and routinely produced and maintained' (38). We have to try to make visible 'What kinds of expectancies make up a "seen but unnoticed" background of common understandings' (44). To do this, ethnomethodology proposes a particular strategy: 'For these background expectancies to come into view one must either be a stranger to the "life as usual" character of everyday scenes or become estranged from them' (37). It therefore seeks to breach the background expectancies to reveal how their structuring role normally goes unnoticed. Garfinkel, for example, asked under-graduate students to view the activities taking place in their homes as if they were newly arrived boarders. In other words, without the background, expectancies that normally help make social interaction understandable. The students' accounts described what they saw as if they did not know the family's history or current circumstances or usual motives and character. What was revealed is that the everyday is full of talk and action that is incomplete. It is by paying attention to these gaps that the structure of the everyday is revealed in the 'common sense' that exists to enable the incomplete to be completed and for everyday life to make enough sense to be taken for granted. If one of the friends in the shopping centre, rather than responding sympathetically to the young man crying, had said, instead, 'I do not understand why you are paying attention to these tears', the whole taken-for-grantedness of the situation might have suddenly required explanation and explanation might have abruptly revealed something of the human constructedness of their interactions. If this had happened, everyday life for a brief moment might have seemed less ordinary and routine.

PHENOMENOLOGICAL SOCIOLOGY

Peter Berger and Thomas Luckmann's central proposition is that 'reality is socially constructed' (1991: 13). To understand every-day life, therefore, we must see it as 'a human product, or, more precisely, an ongoing human production' (69). We are born into a world that existed before our birth; it is a world that was already constituted and organized because of the actions and interactions of other humans who were born before, and often a very long time before us. In this way, then, everyday life is always experienced as pre-structured with already existing rules and regulations, institutions, and social practices. How we understand the world to be meaningful and how these meanings in turn regulate our actions and interactions are embodied and realized in habitualized routines. We experience these as simply how things are and the supposed natural way to respond to situations. As Berger and Luckmann explain, 'All human activity is subject to habitualization. Any action that is repeated frequently becomes cast into a pattern, which can then be reproduced with an economy of effort and which, ipso facto, is apprehended by its performer as that pattern' (70–71).

These processes of habitualization are often institutionalized, involving roles and routines, and 'By playing roles, the individual participates in a social world. By internalizing these roles, the same world becomes subjectively real to him' (91). We might be a mother, a sister, a daughter, a grandmother, a doctor, a professor, a cleaner, or a nurse – each of these roles makes concrete and visible structure of everyday life. Our participation also makes the everyday subjectively real to us but, equally, the institutional roles we play produce the objective institutional reality of everyday life. Our actions and interactions contribute to the ongoing making of everyday life. We make our social worlds, and these take on an objective social reality and it is this objective social reality that in turn enables and constrains our actions and interactions. When, for example, students start at university, the first week is when they are made aware of the expectations of the institution they have entered. To continue to be a student, it is necessary to continually meet these expectations. Very soon most new students will accept these expectations as normal and taken for granted and will act accordingly. But we should not therefore think of this as a structure that only limits and constrains our actions, it also enables. By meeting these expectations, fresh arrivals at university are confirmed in a new social identity – *students.*

What Berger and Luckmann call objectivation is the process whereby we enter human constructions as if they were objective structures (i.e., becoming a student). Everyday life is constructed from 'the objectivations of subjective processes (and meanings)' (34). The more we internalize the objective world outside ourselves, the more the world becomes our world – our everyday reality. If I am angry or happy, there are socially accepted ways to display these feelings. These modes of display are not natural; I have learned and internalized them to the point where they are now fundamental to my reality. They are the 'language' I speak when I act in a particular way. This is the 'language' that is spoken by the friends in the shopping centre.

Objectivation allows me access to the subjectivity of another person. My friend shows me he is angry through his bodily movements and facial expressions. These bodily movements and facial expressions are available for me to use to show another person I am angry. But my friend and I did not invent these ways of acting; we borrowed them from a repertoire of other bodily movements and facial expressions that objectivate subjective feelings. But these borrowings become so embodied and socially embedded that they seem natural and to have been there all the time. As Berger and Luckmann point out, this is because 'my biographical experiences are ongoingly subsumed under general orders of meaning that are both objectively and subjectively real' (54). These objectivations are not only the common currency of everyday life, they are what make everyday life possible. As has already been suggested, 'The reality of everyday life is not only filled with objectivations; it is only possible because of them' (50). Everyday life is full of objects that embody and express the subjectivities and subjective feelings of my fellow citizens and myself. In other words, I am who I am to myself, and to others, through a series of objectivations, and these tend to be guaranteed by various socially recognized and taken-for-granted institutional arrangements.

> Every individual is born into an objective social structure within which he encounters the significant others who are in charge of his socialization. These significant others are imposed upon him. Their definitions of his situation are posited for him as objective reality. He is thus born into not only an objective social structure but also an objective social world. The significant others who mediate this world to him modify it in the course of mediating it. They select aspects of it in accordance with their own location in the social structure, and also by virtue of their individual, biographically rooted idiosyncrasies. The social world is 'filtered' to the individual through this double selectivity. (150)

Phenomenological sociology seeks to show how everyday life is a human construct that everyone confronts at birth as a taken-for-granted realm of routine and habit. Although there seems absolutely nothing here to explain, it is all so obvious and self-evident, the normality of everyday life is a learned normality. Everyone learns what is normal and of course it is not normal at all. All the things I take for granted I have taken from the world around me.

There is individuality, my own biographical situation, in how I have learned these things and how I take them for granted, but they are all socially derived. It is only when something happens to disturb this that I become conscious of these things, otherwise I will continue to follow, without too much ontological concern, the usual everyday routines. The reality of everyday life maintains itself by being embodied in these patterns and routines and is continually reaffirmed by my interactions with others, especially significant others (family and friends), who continually confirm my subjective reality and my sense of place and identity. As Berger and Luckmann explain, 'The reality of everyday life is taken for granted as reality. It does not require additional verification over and beyond its simple presence. It is simply there, as self-evident and compelling facticity. I know that it is real. While I am capable of engaging in doubt about its reality, I am obliged to suspend such doubt as I routinely exist in everyday life' (37). The friends in the shopping centre had no doubts about the normality of what they were doing and what they were doing confirmed and reproduced their understanding of the normality of everyday life, a normality in which consumption in its various forms is simply taken for granted.

ACTOR-NETWORK-THEORY

According to Bruno Latour, actor-network-theory is 'simply another way of being faithful to the insights of ethnomethodology: actors know what they do and we have to learn from them not only what they do, but how and why they do it' (1999: 19). In other words, the everyday[2] is always realized in practice. It appears, for example, in routines and conversations. Like ethnomethodology, actor-network-theory argues that the social should not be thought of as a given, a material domain that can be used to explain human action and interaction; rather it should be seen as something that is assembled, and continually reassembled, by the actions and interactions of humans and non-humans. It should not be understood as a special location or space, but as 'a very peculiar movement of re-association and reassembling' (Latour, 2007: 7).

Latour draws a distinction between ostensive and performative definitions of the social. To see the social as performative rather than ostensive produces a very different concept of everyday life. In an ostensive conceptualization, everyday life can be pointed to, it exists whether or not anyone does anything, whereas in a performative definition, the everyday only exists in its performance; if it stops being performed, it ceases to exist. What the friends were doing in the shopping centre was not acted out against a background of the everyday; in their actions and interactions, the everyday was produced and reproduced. Analysis of the social has to examine it in all its 'ever-changing and provisional shapes' (87). As Latour further explains by analogy, 'If a dancer stops dancing, the dance is finished' (37). If we envisage the social in this way, as 'not a place, a thing, a domain, or a kind of stuff but a provisional movement of new associations' (238), it follows that it cannot be the arena for the staging of social forces, alienation or parapraxes, say, as these are part of the very substance from which the social is constructed. As Latour puts it, 'society is the consequence of associations and not their cause' (ibid.). Therefore, 'it doesn't designate a domain of reality …. It is an association between entities which are in no way recognizably as being social in the ordinary manner, except during that brief moment when they are reshuffled together' (64–65). For example, the text, the tears, the tissues, the hugging, and the words of consolation and then of tipsy anger at the girl-friend are not something staged in everyday life; they are all part of its very fabric. And to modify the point made earlier, without consumers, consumption ceases to exist.

It should not come as any great surprise, therefore, to discover that actor-network-theory is opposed to what it calls the sociology of the social, that is, sociology that regards the social as its stable object of study. As Latour explains, 'the social is something that circulates in a certain way, and not a world beyond to be accessed by the disinterested gaze' (127). Actor-network-theory accuses other sociologists of using the term social to designate two quite different things: 'one of them is the local, face-to-face, naked, unequipped, and dynamic interactions; and the other is a sort of specific force that is supposed to explain why those same temporary face-to-face interactions could become far-reaching and durable' (65). In other words, if the social is assembled from human actions and interactions, it cannot be used to explain these actions and interactions. You cannot have a social explanation of economic activity or language use because it is from such activity and use that the social is assembled. Therefore, to trace the associations of the social we should 'follow the actors themselves' (179). Walking, for example, may be an everyday activity but it is the walking itself and not the walking as enabled and constrained by the social that should be our focus of study. Walking is not contextualized by the social; it is one of the associations that make the social fleetingly visible. As Latour points out, '"social" is not some glue that could fix everything ... it is what is glued together by many other types of connectors' (5). These other connectors are, for example, activities like economics and language use. They cannot be given a social explanation; because they are part of the assemblage, we call the social. Therefore, 'social does not designate a thing among other things ... but a type of connection between things that are not themselves social' (ibid.). Rather than imposing a social explanation on human action and interaction, based on a stable idea of the social, we should try to follow the actors who perform actions that together assemble and reassemble the social. We should not, therefore, decide in advance of empirical research what the social consists of. It is the performance of the social that should be our object of study and not the social as a place where performances are performed. Without such performances, the social would cease to exist. From the perspective of actor-network-theory, the social consists of the many performances that make it visible for analysis. The friends in the shopping centre were such a moment of visibility.

The social is not just people acting and interacting, it is people acting and interacting with objects and objects interacting with each other. Moreover, many of our interactions with other people are mediated through objects of different kinds (see Chapter 5). Whether or not we use a bus or a car to travel to work, wear a suit or casual clothes to meetings, sleep on holiday in a tent or a hotel; these different objects make a difference to the realization of our actions. And because they make a difference, actor-network-theory regards them as 'actors, or more precisely, participants' (71) in our actions. The last time I stayed in St Ives in Cornwall I lived in a lovely apartment overlooking the sea. This was very different from the first occasion when I spent most of the time sleeping on the beach. Both visits involved different 'actors' in my interactions with the Cornish town. Therefore, when we are trying to explain everyday life, we must recognize the actions and interactions of both human and non-human actors. In other words, everyday life is reassembled with the use of objects. 'If action is limited a priori to what "intentional", "meaningful" humans do, it is hard to see how a hammer, a basket, a door closer, a cat, a rug, a mug, a list, or a tag could act' (ibid.). Against the idea of the non-acting object, Latour argues that 'anything that does modify a state of affairs by making a difference is an actor .... Thus, the questions to ask about any agent are simply the following: Does it make a difference in the course of some other agent's action or not?' (ibid.). Beach or lovely apartment makes a difference when spending time in St Ives. If one of the friends had offered her favourite silk handkerchief instead of a tissue, it would have made a difference to the action.

The interaction between actors always takes place in networks. Moreover, we must see actors as networked to each other or we will fail to understand everyday life. In other words, to understand one thing, you must see it in relation to other things; see it as part of a network. Such networks, as we have noted, will often include both humans and non-humans. However, such networks are always performed networks; there is nothing necessarily natural about the network in which a thing is situated; it might also find itself in other networks at other times. Furthermore, it is how something performs or is made to perform within a given network that determines its situated and therefore temporary meaning and significance. For example, if an art gallery exhibited a collection of photographs of a local community, these would temporarily exist in relation to each other, the gallery space, and the local area. Although taken by different photographers for different purposes (a wedding, a sporting event, a mining disaster, an industrial strike), the gallery would situate them all in a network in which these differences of subject and purpose would be diminished, as they would all be, at least temporarily, of significance because of what they tell the gallery audience about the local area. Once removed from the gallery, each photograph would return to other networks. The favourite silk handkerchief is in one network when handed to the young man crying but in another when it was given to the friend by her grandmother and will be in yet another when returned, washed, and ironed. Similarly, the drink passed to the young man in the bar is in a different network from other drinks his friend has bought him, in that it comes with very particular emotional connotations and sense of solidarity.

Objects can be both mediators and intermediaries. Latour insists that we recognize the difference between these two possibilities. Intermediaries convey meaning unchanged, mediators, on the other hand, 'transform, translate, distort, and modify the meaning ... they are supposed to carry' (39). Beach and hotel were both mediators in my experience of St Ives. Most media technologies are first encountered as mediators: that is, our inability to use them properly becomes a meaning in itself as they become actors in our drama of technological inadequacy. However, once we have mastered the technology, they settle down as intermediaries. If the technology breaks down, it has the potential to become a mediator again, once more an actor in the theatre of our everyday existence. When, for example, I give a lecture, the PowerPoint I use in the lecture theatre mediates between the students and myself: the technology is fundamental to the experience of our interaction. In other words, the interaction between us involves technology and this technology does not just work as an intermediary, it acts as a mediator – it makes a difference that my words are on PowerPoint and not just spoken. Similarly, the favourite silk handkerchief is potentially an intermediary like the tissues offered by the other friends. But because the young man knows it is his friend's favourite handkerchief, it becomes a mediator in that it conveys an additional meaning of special friendship and the possible promise of more.

According to Latour, a network is 'a string of actions where each participant is treated as a full-blown mediator' (128). In a network, all the actors act: there is movement not between intermediaries but between mediators. 'As soon as actors are treated not as intermediaries but as mediators, they render the movement of the social visible' (ibid.). In a network, there is not the transport of causality between intermediaries but a series of connections in which actors make other actors act. The remote control does not cause me to become a lazy person; it permits me to become one. There is a relationship between my behaviour and what the infrared signal allows, but it is not a relationship of simple cause and effect. It is an actor in a drama of laziness. Moreover, quite simply, an actor that does not act is not an actor.

If we extend this to thinking about everyday life, it draws our attention to difficulties with this concept. As we have seen, everyday life is itself often seen as a substance, a kind of domain in which certain routines take place. But perhaps we would be better to see it as something fluid that can only be seen in the fleeting moments of its associations, recognizing that these associations always involve both humans and non-humans? To explain everyday life, therefore, we should not begin by thinking we know what it is. Instead, it must be assembled as an object of study from the evidence of its existence. Furthermore, we will not understand the involvement of objects if we insist on drawing a clear distinction between material and social action and interaction. According to Latour,

> any human course of action might weave together in a matter of minutes, for instance, a shouted order to lay a brick, the chemical connection of cement with water, the force of a pulley unto a rope with a movement of the hand, the strike of a match to light a cigarette offered by a co-worker, etc. Here, the apparently reasonable division between material and social becomes just what is obfuscating any enquiry on how a collective action is possible. (74)

The weaving together of both material and social, that is, human-to-human, object-to-object, and human-to-object actions and interactions, is what assembles what other sociologists call society and everyday life.

A common way to think of everyday life is as a relationship between structure and agency: everyday life is a structure that enables and constrains everyday human action and interaction. One of the things actor-network-theory does is complicate this relationship. From the perspective of actor-network-theory, the implications for a concept of everyday life are quite clear. We cannot assume the everyday as an arena for the actions and interactions of everyday life. Such a tautology would confuse cause and effect, as it is the actions and interactions of everyday life ('effect') that produce what we think of as the enabling and constraining structure of the everyday ('cause'). But is this really true? We could make a counterargument in which we insist that the everyday always already exists as a historical/temporal structure of rules and expectations that every new everyday action and interaction must encounter and accommodate. The relationship is not one of cause and effect but historical and dialectical. What is presented as cause and what is presented as effect cannot simply be reversed; they must be seen as existing together in a dialectical and historical relationship. In other words, everyday life is a structure that enables and constrains agency while at the same time being a structure that is continually reproduced by the agency of new actions and interaction. To argue that the structure of the everyday enables and constrains the agency of the everyday is to forget that the structure itself consists of the very agency it is claimed it enables and constrains. Therefore, although it is true that when the dancer stops dancing, the dance is finished, it is also true that without a concept of dance, the dancer would never start dancing (or, at the very least, we would not know she was dancing). Put another way, actors make theatre, but theatre also makes actors. The relationship is historical and dialectical. 'We make history, but not in circumstances chosen by ourselves' (Marx, 1977: 10). In other words, historical circumstances always precede new acts of history-making and because these already exist they enable and constrain the new acts. This is not a relationship of cause and effect, but a relationship in which structure (made up of acts of agency) enables and constrains new forms of agency, while at the same time being reproduced by such actions and interactions.

PRACTICE THEORY

Practice theory works with many of the assumptions that inform symbolic interactionism ethnomethodology, phenomenological sociology, and actor-network-theory. A practice consists of an interconnected series of both physical and mental activities, in which bodily actions (ways of doing something) are combined with mental actions (modes of interpretation, learned assumptions, presuppositions, and expectations). As Theodore Schatzki explains, practices are 'a temporally unfolding and spatially disperse nexus of doings and sayings' (quoted in Warde, 2017: 82). According to Schatzki, the sayings and doings are connected in three ways: '(1) through understandings, for example, of what to say and do; (2) through explicit rules, principles, precepts and instructions; and

(3) through what I call "teleaffective" structures embracing ends, projects, tasks, purposes, beliefs, emotions and moods' (ibid.). We find all of these in the example of how the friends respond to the young man crying in the shopping centre.

According to practice theory, consumption is not itself a practice but something we do as part of a practice. How and what we consume is inseparable from the social practices we engage in. Eating a pie and drinking Bovril on a Saturday afternoon was traditionally part of the practice of watching football in England and yet unlikely to happen today if we are watching a game on TV. Similarly, eating popcorn at the local multiplex can be replicated when watching a film at home, but it will usually be done with a knowing reference to what one does when going to the cinema. What happens within a practice is never dictated by the practice itself. We can locate reading in a range of different practices and find that, in each case, consumption is quite different. Reading for pleasure on a summer's day in a back garden or local park is very different from reading for an exam in a university library. In both cases, we are reading, and it could even be the same book, but each practice determines how we read and the consequences that might follow from it: (a) I might discuss what I read with family and friends or (b) I might make notes for an upcoming exam. If, to return to our ongoing example, the young woman had offered a tissue rather than a silk handkerchief, the practice of friendship would have been quite different. Therefore, to understand consumption, we need to examine not the activities of individual consumers, but consumption as located in a social practice. Shopping, for example, is a practice that combines certain physical activities with a range of mental actions. Each individual shopper makes manifest the practice of shopping. When we engage in such performances, we become what Andreas Reckwitz calls 'carriers of practice' (2002: 250).[3] As already noted, shopping requires shoppers, but it is the practice of shopping which makes us into shoppers. Our identity as a shopper only becomes manifest in the social practice of shopping. A shopper is thus the carrier of both the physical and mental activities of a practice that defines them as someone shopping. As Reckwitz explains, 'A practice is thus a routinized way in which bodies are moved, objects are handled, subjects are treated, things are described, and the world is understood' (2002: 250). Shopping is a practice in which the mental and physical routines of individual shoppers are reproduced. But, as we saw in the example of the friends in the shopping centre, going shopping involves many different forms of consumption.

Like the other approaches discussed in this chapter, practice theory invites us to rethink structure and agency. It is not a relationship in which agents can ignore structures, nor is it one in which structures dictate what agents can do. Rather, structures are recursively reproduced in the activities of agents. Therefore, our critical focus should not fix upon the individual actor, nor on a determining structure, but on the practices which both enable and constrain human activity. Shopping is not a structure which dictates how a shopper must act, nor are shoppers free agents who individually define what shopping is. Rather, shopping is a practice made manifest by the physical and mental activities of shoppers. In practice theory, therefore, structures only become manifest when agents become carriers of social practices. As Elisabeth Shove maintains, 'dominant rhetorics and reasonings "pin" practice in place, that practices move as legitimizing rationales change and that these adjust in response to the reformulation of persistent structural concerns. At the same time, I insist on the point that it is the routinization of practice that gives these reasonings their collective power' (2003: 95). Speaking or writing a language is a practice. Like any practice, language both enables and constrains. It enables us to communicate, while at the same time constraining what we can say. Moreover, its visibility as an institution is made manifest and reproduced in acts of speaking and writing. Sometimes how we formulate what we say may bring about a change more widely in the use of the language. Youth subcultures are the obvious example of where this often happens. The friends in the shopping centre are part of an ongoing redefinition of what 'going shopping' means.

A practice is both a performance, something done (agency), and a pattern of doings (structure). Everyday life exists in the performances of the *doings* of individuals, which in turn produce and reproduce a pattern of *doings*. It is this pattern of *doings* that solidifies into habit and routine. Elizabeth Shove, Mika Pantzar, and Matt Watson distinguish between 'practice-as-performance and practice-as-entity' (2012: 7). Shopping exists as a recognizably series of entities – shops, commodities, salespeople, etc. But it also exists as a set of performances, what we call 'going shopping'. As they explain,

> It is through performance, through the immediacy of doing, that the 'pattern' provided by the practice-as-an-entity is filled out and reproduced. It is only through successive moments of performance that the interdependencies between elements which constitute the practice as entity are sustained over time. Accordingly, [a practice] only exists and endures because of countless recurrent enactments, each reproducing the interdependencies of which the practice is comprised.
>
> (ibid.)

While there can be little doubt that shopping is often an articulation of scripted practices, this does not mean that agency always disappears beneath the dead weight of structure. We must remember that in this instance structure consists of an accumulation of agency. In other words, scripted practices consist of the doings of agency that over time become the routines and habits of structure. What was once new and perhaps unusual becomes normalized and embedded in habit and routine. The young man being comforted is an example of practice-as-performance, which in turn produces friendship as practice-as-entity.

A great deal of consumption is inconspicuous. As Alan Warde explains, 'most consumption is habitual and non-reflective' (2017: 73).[4] It exists, without much notice being taken, within the socially constructed customs and habits of everyday life. It passes almost unnoted and unnoticed, unless, of course, we are foreign to these customs and habits. When this happens, what seems natural to *them* can seem very strange to *us*. Shove argues, in a very compelling phrase, that practice theory entails the investigation of 'the constitution of normality and the dynamics of habit and routine' (2003: 1). Being repetitive and recursive does not make it 'natural'. Routine and habit are learned patterns of behaviour. As Shove also points out, 'Normality is made of what people normally do' (115). A failure to meet certain social conventions is often regarded as an inability to be normal. If the friends had not comforted their friend, this would have been a breach of their sense of 'normality'.[5]

NOTES

1 For an entertaining non-sociological account of a version of the popular perception of everyday life as a 'sociologist's paradise', see John Cooper Clarke's performance poem, 'Beasley Street' (*The Very Best of John Cooper Clarke*, Sony).

2 In the chapter, I have assumed that 'everyday', 'everyday life', and 'the social' are more or less the same. I have therefore used the first two interchangeably. I have only used 'the social' when it is essential to an explanation of Latour's meaning.

3 Sounds remarkably like a very influential theory of ideology developed by Louis Althusser (see Althusser, 2019; Storey, 2021a).

4 Warde's claim that 'most consumption is habitual and non-reflective' (2017: 73) is open to challenge. Although I might buy a sandwich because I need to eat, what I buy will depend on certain considerations: for example, how much money I can spend, where I intend to eat, who I am with, what I intend to do after eating. These things involve some reflection. Therefore, while the need to eat is habitual and non-reflective, the process of eating might be quite different.

5 If we had discussed the example of the friends in the shopping centre on a Saturday afternoon in our exploration of Butler's theory of performativity (see Chapter 3), we might have had to consider the role a particular toxic version of masculine identity might have played in what happened. Some of the friends of the young man crying might have secretly mocked him for being unmanly, a sign he did not really deserve his girlfriend and that the end of the relationship was therefore inevitable.

SOCIOLOGY AFTER CULTURAL STUDIES

In this chapter, I discuss the contribution of cultural studies to the sociology of consumption. Drawing on the work of one of the founding figures, Raymond Williams, I begin with a brief overview of the theoretical foundations of cultural studies. This is followed by a discussion of consumption as found in the work of another of the founders of cultural studies, Richard Hoggart. Then, drawing on work I have published elsewhere, I outline a case study on how acts of reading, often unacknowledged as consumption, are fundamental to an assessment of what we might call the politics of utopian fiction (including dystopian and anti-utopian).

CULTURAL STUDIES

As the name implies, the primary focus of cultural studies is the study of culture. To fully understand this, we must understand what culture means in cultural studies. After outlining the cultural studies' concept of culture, I will then explain how this informs its understanding of consumption. In *Culture*, written for the Fontana New Sociology series, Williams outlined what he called culture as 'a realized signifying system' (1981: 12), arguing that it is fundamental to the shaping and holding together of all ways of life, insisting that culture defined in this way should be seen 'as essentially involved in all forms of social activity' (13). As he further explains, 'the social organisation of culture, as a realised signifying system, is embedded in a whole range of activities, relations and institutions, of which some are manifestly "cultural"' (209). While there is more to life than signifying systems, it is

DOI: 10.4324/9781003224471-7

nevertheless the case that 'it would ... be wrong to suppose that we can ever usefully discuss a social system without including, as a central part of its practice, its signifying systems, on which, as a system, it fundamentally depends' (207). In other words, signification is fundamental to all human activities, including practices of consumption.[1]

Culture, therefore, as defined by Williams, is not something restricted to the arts or to different forms of intellectual production, it is an aspect of all human practice. For example, if I pass a name card to someone in China, the polite way to do it is with two hands. If I pass it with one hand, I may cause offence. This is clearly a matter of culture. However, the culture is not simply in the social act, nor is it just in the materiality of the card; it is in the realized meaning of both act and card. In other words, there is not anything essentially polite about using two hands; nor is there anything essentially polite about exchanging a name card; using two hands to pass the card has been made to signify politeness. Signification has become embodied in a material object and a social practice. Therefore, as Williams insists, 'Signification, the social creation of meanings ... is ... a practical material activity' (1977: 34). It is a social practice that requires human agency. It is not something abstract; it is embedded in human action and interaction. To share a culture, therefore, according to this definition, is to interpret the world, make it meaningful, and experience it as meaningful in recognizably similar ways. When Williams said that 'culture is ordinary' (1989; originally 1958), he was drawing attention to the fact that meaning making is not the privileged activity of the few, but something in which we are all involved. However, this does not of course mean that we are all involved in it in the same way; meaning making, like all social activities, is often entangled in relations of power. While we may all be involved in the making of meanings, it is also the case that some meanings and the people who make them have more power than other people and other meanings. Therefore, signifying systems consist of both shared and contested meanings. Culture is where we share and contest meanings of ourselves, of each other, and of the social worlds in which we live.

Williams' argument is informed by Antonio Gramsci's concept of hegemony. Gramsci uses hegemony to describe processes of power in which a dominant group does not merely rule by force but leads by consent: it exerts 'intellectual and moral leadership' (2019: 69). Hegemony involves a specific kind of consensus, a consensus in which a social group presents its own specific interests as the general interests of the society as a whole; it turns the particular into the general. Hegemony works by the transformation of potential antagonism into simple difference.[2] This works in part through the circulation of signification that reinforces dominance and subordination by seeking to fix the meaning of social relations. As Williams explains, hegemony 'is a lived system of meanings and values …. It thus constitutes a sense of reality for most people …. It is … in the strongest sense a "culture" [understood as a realized signifying system], but a culture which has also to be seen as the lived dominance and subordination of particular classes' (1977: 110).

Hegemony involves the attempt to saturate the social with meanings that support the prevailing structures of power. In hegemonic situations, subordinate groups appear to actively support and subscribe to values, ideals, objectives, etc., which incorporate them into relations of dominance and subordination. However, hegemony, as Williams observes, 'does not just passively exist as a form of dominance. It has continually to be renewed, recreated, defended, and modified. It is also continually resisted, limited, altered, challenged' (112). Therefore, although it is characterized by high levels of consensus, it is never without conflict; that is, there is always resistance. However, hegemony seeks to arrest the proliferation of meanings; it seeks to reduce signification to meanings that can be controlled. For it to remain successful, conflict and resistance must always be channelled and contained – rearticulated in the interests of the dominant.

But we should not see hegemony as another term for social control or dominant ideology, sweeping all resistance into the waste bin of power. Hegemony is an active process, *hegemonization*, the making and remaking of 'common sense' in defence of the prevailing structures of power. And because it is an active process, it always implies its other, *anti-hegemonization*. In other words, hegemony consists not just of consensus and coercion, but of 'a certain compromise equilibrium' (2019: 69) between incorporation and resistance. As Gramsci points out,

The 'normal' exercise of hegemony on the now classical terrain of the parliamentary regime is characterised by the combination of force and consent, which balance each other reciprocally, without force predominating excessively over consent. Indeed, the attempt is always made to ensure that force will appear to be based on the consent of the majority, expressed by the so-called organs of public opinion – newspapers and associations – which, therefore, in certain situations, are artificially multiplied.

(ibid.)

Language use works in much the same way as the compromise equilibrium of hegemony. Languages exist as both performance and system. It is a structure which enables agency, but to make sense, the agency it enables must remain within the current rules of the structure. Consumption works in a similar way. While we have some choice over what we consume, we rarely have choice over what is made available to be consumed. Again, there is always 'a certain compromise equilibrium' between production and consumption, between structure and agency.

There are two conclusions we can draw from Williams' concept of culture as a realized signifying system, and both, I want to suggest, point to the importance of consumption as an object of study. First, although the world exists in all its enabling and constraining materiality outside culture, it is only in culture as a realized signifying system that the world can be made to mean. In other words, signification has a 'performative effect' (Austin, 1962; Butler, 1993, 1999, and Chapter 3); it helps construct the realities it appears only to describe. Moreover, meanings inform and organize social action. As Stuart Hall explains,

Meanings … regulate and organise our conduct and practices – they help to set the rules, norms and conventions by which social life is ordered and governed. They are …, therefore, what those who wish to govern and regulate the conduct and ideas of others seek to structure and shape.

(1997: 4)

The second conclusion we can draw from seeing culture as a realized signifying system concerns the potential for struggle over meaning. As discussed in Chapter 1, given that different meanings can be ascribed to the same 'sign' (that is, anything that can be made to signify), meaning making is always a potential site of struggle. The making of meaning is always confronted by what Volosinov identifies as the 'multi-accentuality of the sign' (1973: 23). Rather than being inscribed with a single meaning, a sign can be articulated with different 'accents'; that is, it can be made to mean different things in different contexts, with different effects of power. The sign, therefore, is always a potential site of 'differently oriented social interests' (ibid.) and is often in practice 'an arena of ... struggle' (ibid.). Those with power seek 'to make the sign uni-accentual' (ibid.): they seek to make what is multi-accentual appear as if it could only ever be uni-accentual. In other words, a 'sign' is not the issuing source of meaning but a site where the articulation of meaning (variable meanings) can be produced as it is rearticulated in specific contexts. The different ways of making something signify are not an innocent game of semantics; they are a significant part of a power struggle over what might be regarded as 'normal' or 'correct' – an example of the politics of signification. It is about who can claim the power and authority to define social reality to make the world (and the things in it) mean in particular ways and with specific effects of power. All attempts to fix the meaning of consumption are an example of the politics of signification.

Although cultural studies views consumption as a form of 'agency', it is critically aware that agency always takes place within the confines of specific structures. Agents are mostly aware of what they are actively doing when they consume; to understand this, we need to undertake forms of ethnographic study. But agents may not be totally aware of the full significance of the structures in which they consume. Now this is not to suggest that agents are always passively positioned by the structures enabling and constraining the limits of consumption, but it is to make clear that to understand the structural conditions in which specific practices of consumption may take place, we need to always frame the research theoretically. In doing this, we recognize that studying consumption is not the same as the experience of the consumption we study. In other words, we should not pretend that our study is simply an innocent replication of the object of our study. If it were the same, what would be the point of ethnographic research?

An ethnography is not undertaken to simply describe but to understand something about consumption. In Paul Willis' classic cultural studies text *Learning to Labour* (1977), a study of working-class kids consuming and not consuming education, he ultimately knows more about the full consequences of their schooling than they do and after reading the book, so do we. This is not to patronize or not to take seriously the subjects of ethnography, but it is to recognize that we are always seeking to do is more than describe and replicate the self-knowledge of the consumers we study. As sociologist Anthony Giddens observes in a discussion of Willis' study, the working-class boys are aware of their location in the power structures of the school and react against this by various acts of rebellion. What they are less conscious of are the structures of power outside the school and how these might relate to the power structure of the school. Moreover, their success in resisting the power structure of the school results in them receiving an education that directs them to unskilled and unrewarding labour. In this way, as Giddens observes, their actions facilitate 'the reproduction of some general features of capitalist-industrial labour. Constraint, in other words, is shown to operate through the active involvement of the agents concerned, not as some force of which they are passive recipients' (1984: 289). The boys would soon become all too aware of how their 'resistance' to education prepared them for specific patterns of work. What Willis's theoretical framework brings to the situation is an understanding of how their actions also contribute to the structural needs of industrial capitalism and the reproduction of class inequality. As social anthropologists George Marcus and Michael Fischer observe,

> Willis is explicitly concerned both with the remarkable insights of his working-class subjects about the nature of capitalist process and with the limited self-understanding that they display concerning the ironic implications of their rebellious behaviour at school. In learning to resist the school environment, his lads establish the kinds of attitudes and practices that lock them into their class position, foreclosing the possibility of upward mobility. Resistance is thus an intimate part of the process of reproducing capitalist-class relations. The linkage of the local situation of cultural learning and resistance at the level of the

school to the situation of labor in capitalist production at the level of the shop floor is thus one of unintended consequences.

(1986: 82)

It is simply wrong, therefore, to claim that cultural studies, in its rejection of the absolute determining power of structures, views consumption as 'a realm of individual agency and choice' (Warde, 2017: 42). Rejecting the idea that people consume like dupes, does not mean that they are free agents in their choices. If we are looking for a guiding principle in cultural studies on matters of consumption, it can be found in Marx's dialectic of *making* and *circumstances*. As he explains, 'Men make their own history, but they do not make it just as they please; they do make it under circumstances chosen by themselves, but under circumstances directly encountered, given and transmitted from the past' (1977: 10). To paraphrase Marx, individuals consume, but they do not consume just as they please; they do not consume under circumstances chosen by themselves, but under circumstances directly encountered, given, and transmitted from the past. In other words, our consumption choices are often not individual at all but are shaped by our social and cultural location. When cultural studies insists that consumption is an active process, it is not claiming, as certain critics like to suggest, that it is something free of constraints or determinations, what Marx called *circumstances*. Lots of things may curtail our freedom to choose what we consume. Moreover, what counts as utility or satisfaction in matters of consumption is often a question of society and culture. If consumption was simply a matter of individual preferences, we would not see the clustering of patterns of consumption connected to, for example, ethnicity, 'race', class, or gender.

What cultural studies insists is that consumption always finds itself in a relationship with production that parallels other relationships – critical homologies – that help us understand consumption/production relations (see Table 7.1). As Williams maintains, 'we have to discover the nature of a practice and then its conditions' (1980: 47). Working with this idea, I would suggest, leads to a critical perspective in which production is seen to provide not a mechanistically determining factor, but the conditions of existence for the social practice of consumption. Therefore, while it is clearly important to locate the commodities people consume within the

Table 7.1 Critical homologies

Structure	Agency
Making	Circumstances
Incorporation	Resistance
Uni-accentuality	Multi-accentuality
Use-value	Exchange-value
Production	Consumption

field of the economic conditions of their existence, it is clearly insufficient to do this and think you have also already analysed important questions of appropriation and use. It is simplistic, and, moreover, it is analytically disabling, to assume that practices of consumption must mirror the 'intentions' of production. The capitalist commodity has a double existence, as both use-value and exchange-value. Crucial to this argument is the fact that 'the use-value of a commodity cannot be known in advance of investigation of actual use of the commodity' (Lovell, 2019: 596). As Marx observed, how a commodity is used 'may arise from the stomach' or from the 'imagination' (1976a: 125). Furthermore, as Terry Lovell points out, commodities

> have different use values for the individuals who use and purchase them than they have for the capitalists who produce and sell them, and in turn, for capitalism as a whole. We may assume that people do not purchase these … artifacts in order to expose themselves to bourgeois ideology … but to satisfy a variety of different wants which can only be guessed at in the absence of analysis and investigation. There is no guarantee that the use-value of the … object for its purchaser will even be compatible with its utility to capitalism as bourgeois ideology.
>
> (2019: 598)

As Lovell's comments suggest, it is important to distinguish between the power of the producers of commodities and the power of their influence. Too often the two are conflated, but they are not necessarily the same. If our focus is consumption, then our focus must be consumption as it is experienced and not as it should be experienced as already determined in a prior analysis of the relations of production.

THE USES OF LITERACY

Hoggart inherited from Leavisism (see Storey, 2021a) the assumption that working-class culture consisted solely of the commodities produced by the culture industries. Therefore, all that was required to understand, say, the books read by the working class was an analysis of how as commodities they were produced for consumption. Hoggart's *The Uses of Literacy* challenges this twofold assumption. Throughout Part One of the book, and contrary to the argument that underpins Part Two, there is a clear distinction to be made between working-class culture and mass culture.[3] There is a relationship, but they are not the same: working-class culture is actively made from the consumption of a repertoire of texts and practices produced by the culture industries. Hoggart repeatedly attempts to mark a clear difference between mass culture and working-class culture:

[We have to try to see the way] mass publications connect with commonly accepted attitudes, how they are altering those attitudes, and how they are meeting resistance. (19)

[T]hese tendencies [the circulation of mass culture] are meeting resistance.

(1990: 174)

[T]hose who do ['sing or listen to these songs'], often make the songs better than they really are. (231)

[P]eople often read them [newspapers and magazines] in their own way. So that even there they are less affected than the extent of their purchases would seem to indicate.

(ibid.)

It is commonly assumed … that working-class people are more deeply affected by their reading than they are. (238)

[T]he resistances [to mass culture] I have repeatedly stressed. (246)

People are not living lives which are imaginatively as poor as a mere reading of their literature would suggest. (324)

Underpinning these various claims is a division between mass culture as something imposed for profit and working-class consumption as a form of appropriation, resistance, and making. The distinction was very important to Hoggart, as we find him making it elsewhere, and it is crucial to the development of cultural studies. In his inaugural professorial lecture at Birmingham University in 1963, 'Schools of English and Contemporary Society', which was in effect the founding moment of the Centre for Contemporary Cultural Studies (CCCS), he called for 'a little more humility about what audiences actually take from unpromising material' (1970: 242). In volume 1 of his autobiography, he makes a similar point, repeating the claim that much would be learned by considering 'what people might make of that material' (1991: 135).

Whereas the Leavisites condemned the products of the culture industries for what they do to those who consumed them, Hoggart in Part One locates the products in actual practices of consumption and the making of culture. Put simply, this is the difference between reading the impact of a commodity from the commodity itself or how it was produced and reading impact from how it is consumed. Let us consider one of Hoggart's most famous examples, a coach trip to the seaside:

> after that a fanning out in groups. But rarely far from one another, because they know their part of the town and their bit of beach, where they feel at home .... They have a nice walk past the shops; perhaps a drink; a sit in a deck chair eating an ice cream or sucking mint humbugs; a great deal of loud laughter - at Mrs Johnson insisting on a paddle with her dress tucked in her bloomers, at Mrs Henderson pretending she has 'got off' with the deck chair attendant, or in the queue at the ladies' lavatory. Then there is the buying of presents for the family, a big meat-tea, and the journey home with a stop for drinks on the way .... The driver knows exactly what is expected of him as he steers his warm, fuggy, and singing community back to the town; for his part he gets a large tip, collected during the run through the last few miles of town streets. (147–148)

Hoggart argues that these activities can be read like a text for their patterns of signification. He makes three important points. First, this

Table 7.2 At the seaside: mass culture and working-class culture

Mass culture (produced by the culture industries for the people)	Working-class culture (produced by the people from mass culture)
Seaside resort (facilities, etc.)	What people do at the seaside
Mass culture	Working-class culture

is a self-made culture produced by the working class; second, it is therefore a communal culture of the working class; third, it is a culture that is an expression of working-class values and experience – it has been made to articulate working-classness. We can add that consumption is clearly inseparable from all three points.

Again, there is a clear distinction here between mass culture produced by the culture industries for the working class and working-class culture produced by the working class from the texts and practices of mass culture. The seaside resort, its general facilities, should not be confused with what people do at the seaside; what they make from what is made available for their consumption (see Table 7.2).

Hoggart also gives the example of popular songs. He defends their working-class consumption and appropriation in terms that would soon become central to the project of cultural studies at Birmingham and beyond. Songs succeed, he argues, 'no matter how much Tin Pan Alley plugs them' (159), only if they can be made to meet the emotional requirements of their working-class audience. Although the songs are the product of the culture industries, some are made to become part of working-class culture. For example, he describes 'After the Ball is Over' as 'a commercial song taken over by the people; but they have taken it on their own terms, and so it is not for them as poor a thing as it might have been' (162). The distinction he makes between mass culture and working-class culture in Part One of *The Uses of Literacy* is crucial to the founding of cultural studies and processes of consumption are central to his argument. So, we can add to Table 7.3 Hoggart's distinction between working-class culture and mass culture. Again, another example of what Gramsci calls a 'compromise equilibrium' (2019: 69).

It is a commonplace in textbook histories of cultural studies to suggest that, as it developed, it moved quickly beyond Hoggart's

Table 7.3 Critical homologies

Structure	Agency
Making	Circumstances
Incorporation	Resistance
Uni-accentuality	Multi-accentuality
Exchange-value	Use-value
Production	Consumption
Mass culture	Working-class culture

founding contribution. I want to suggest a slightly different argument, one in which the moving beyond Hoggart was a move facilitated by his founding contribution. In other words, the move was enabled and encouraged by the foundations already laid by Hoggart. Michael Green refers to what he calls a shift 'from Hoggart to Gramsci' (1996: 49). Fundamental to this shift was what he describes as 'Hoggart's remarkably enduring formulation'. He then quotes Hoggart,

> I have therefore taken one fairly homogeneous group of working-class people, have tried to evoke the atmosphere, the quality, of their lives by describing their setting and their attitudes. Against this background may be seen how much the more generally diffused appeals of the mass publications connect with commonly accepted attitudes, how they are altering those attitudes and how they are meeting resistance.
>
> (Hoggart, 1990: 18–19)

What Green is suggesting (a suggestion with which I fully concur) is that the CCCS did not reject Hoggart for Gramsci; the Italian Marxist's work was more easily assimilated into the Centre's work because Part One of *The Uses of Literacy* already existed there. So, when Green writes about a shift from Hoggart to Gramsci, what he is describing is not so much a supersession as a building upon. In other words, we must distinguish between *post*-Hoggart (which involves going beyond him) and post-*Hoggart* (building upon his work). My argument is that when the work of Gramsci was introduced into the CCCS, this involved a move that is best described as post-*Hoggart*.

CONSUMING UTOPIAN FICTION

What follows is a sociological speculation about politics and reading. In critical discussions, it is quite common to encounter the argument that utopian fiction (including dystopian and anti-utopian) is political. While I agree and share Fredric Jameson's insistence that 'the political perspective [is] the absolute horizon of all reading and all interpretation' (1981: 17), too often this means little more than a critical commentary on what Bertolt Brecht calls 'solutions *on paper*' (1980: 72; italics in original). We can argue endlessly that this or that text is political, but unless someone reads it and acts upon what they read, this is a politics that will hardly trouble the prevailing structures of power. In other words, consumption is central to the production of politics beyond the text. Therefore, the primary argument here is that if utopian fiction has a politics, its fundamental location is in social practices of reading. Contrary to a particular common sense, a popular fetishism, books do not change the world. We might point to the *Bible*, the *Quran*, or the *Communist Manifesto* and say these books changed the world, when what we really mean is that the readers of these books made the change. Therefore, a discussion of the politics of utopian fiction must be a discussion of reading and readers. Not readers as proposed by textuality, but actual, material readers who pick up books and act on what they read. As Williams pointed out in *Marxism and Literature*, the production of meaning is 'a practical material activity' (1977: 34), and in the best traditions of cultural studies, I will attempt to show how reading utopian fiction may work to make meaning material and social and therefore available for politics.

Production and textuality have been the critical focus of most studies of utopian fiction. The assumption being that meaning is produced by an author and embodied in a text. The part played by a reader is to receive this meaning as accurately as possible. The only readers that matter are authors, critics, and academics. In this argument, the materiality of the text is confused with the meaning of the text. Although a text has a materiality which limits how it might be read, it does not have meaning other than when it is read. Of course, a text can exist perfectly well in all its materiality without a reader, but for meaning to be produced, a text must be consumed by a reader. We should think of this as a division between materiality and meaning. As Ursula K Le Guin points out, 'The unread story is not a story; it is little black marks on wood pulp. The reader, reading it, makes it live' (quoted in Willis, 2018: 2). This is very similar to Marx's point about consumption: 'a product only obtains its last finish in consumption .... For example, a dress becomes a real dress only in the act of being worn; a house which is uninhabited is in fact no real house; in other words, a product, as distinct from a mere natural object, proves itself as such, becomes a product, only in consumption' (1976b: 19). This is the difference between a material object and an object made meaningful in acts of consumption. To understand the production of meaning, we must fully distinguish between the materiality of a text and the meaning of a text. The first is written by an author and distributed by a publisher, while the second is made by a reader in a social practice of reading.[4] The first is an object of production, the second comes into being only in acts of consumption. When I buy a copy of Marge Piercy's *Woman on the Edge of Time*, I carry home a material object; it is only when I sit down to read it that I begin to produce meaning from the book's materiality. This does not mean that the meaning is a subjective event, leading to the suggestion that any meaning can be subjectively imposed upon a text. Although we approach a text with preconceived ideas, what we always encounter is the materiality of the text itself (particular words ordered in particular ways, which allow the reader to recognize a difference between, say, Jack London's *The Iron Heel* and *The Parable of the Sower* by Octavia E Butler). An understanding of a text is therefore always a process in which preconceived ideas are confronted (and perhaps modified) by the materiality of the text. Authors may have intentions, and texts certainly have material structures, but meaning is never a simple activation of what already exists in a text. Meaning is a production made in consumption in an interaction between text and reader and cannot be defined outside this encounter. It is like a dialogue of questions and answers: we ask questions of a text, but if a satisfactory understanding is to be achieved, we must always remain open to the answers it gives to the questions we ask. Both text and reader bring something to the encounter. Moreover, politics and the making of meaning are inseparable. Therefore, what meanings are made is vital to an understanding of the politics of utopian fiction.

Gregory Claeys claims to know the meaning of *Nineteen Eighty-Four* by knowing George Orwell's intentions. He even complains that Isaac Deutscher rejects intentionality. As he explains, 'It does not help that Deutscher asserted that a "book like 1984 may be used without much regard for the author's intentions"' (2018: 35). Claeys seems to think that Orwell's intentions determine and guarantee the meaning of the novel. He seems to have no idea that a book can in fact be used without much regard for an author's intentions. Timothy Leary once remarked of Aldous Huxley's utopian novel *Island*, 'It is a great book. It will become a greater book' (1993: 255). He never elaborated on what he meant by this. He could have simply been repeating the old cliché that great books get better with time, but I think he was talking about how the countercul-ture's use of lysergic acid diethylamide (LSD) would generate a particular way of reading the book (see Storey, 2019). The novel itself would not change, but the context in which it was read would and this would in turn change how it was read. Joanna Russ was once accused by her colleague Elly Bulkin of not paying enough attention to women writers of colour. In response, Russ read Zora Neale Hurston's *Their Eyes Were Watching God*. Her initial response was not positive. She found it 'thin' and 'episodic' and 'clearly inferior to the great central tradition of Western literature' (Russ; quoted in Willis, 2018: 114). However, after reading more litera-ture by women of colour and examples of black literary criticism, she returned to Hurston's novel. 'It was astonishing how much it had improved in the meantime' (ibid.). It no longer seemed 'thin' and 'episodic' (or she re-evaluated what she had previously under-stood by these terms). But, of course, what has changed was not Hurston's novel but the context in which it was read by Russ. It is what she brings to the novel that changes how she reads it. There-fore, knowing what the author intended tells us very little about the political outcomes of reading utopian fiction. What readers bring to a text is far more important than what an author intends. Discontents and desires, expectations and anticipations, crowd in upon the materiality of the text as meaning is produced in the social practice of reading. How we read changes as our context of reading changes. Ruth Levitas' comment on reading and rereading is very telling, 'I originally read *Island* in the late 1960s. When I returned to it in 2012, fifty years after its publication, it seemed less appealing. I was shocked by its sexism, misogyny and homophobia, none of which I had originally noticed' (2014: 260). I am not sure of the context in which she originally read Huxley's novel, but when I first read it in the early 1970s, it was as 'a book about acid' to be read alongside *The Doors of Perception* and almost anything by Herman Hesse. Rereading it for *Consuming Utopia* (Storey, 2021b) was a very different experience indeed.

When it comes to meaning, context is almost everything. Meaning is only ever partial, always historical and is something that must be made – things do not mean by themselves. Objects are mute. Meaning is always made. So, when someone tells you, 'It is just what it means', always think critically according to whom, for what, when? A context is a historically constituted array of discourses (see discussion of discourse in Chapter 1) that enable and constrain what a text might be made to mean. The word context comes into English in the late fifteenth century. It derives from the Latin words contextus, meaning to join together, and contexere, meaning to weave together. A context, then, always in part produced by a reader, consists of the other texts that are woven together with the text in question to produce meaning. Although the meaning of a specific text is a co-production between text and reader and does not exist prior to this encounter, other meanings of the text, known to the reader, may influence how a text is read. However, we should not think of contexts as only texts being joined with other texts. When we try to make sense of a text, we always bring to it a set of presuppositions which provide a framework for our analysis. As they are woven together around the text to be analysed, they help construct a specific context for our understanding of the text. In these ways, then, contexts are both the co-texts of a text (the texts we join to a particular text) and the presuppositions brought to the text by a reader (the ideas we weave around a particular text in order to understand it). The first is an extension of the text in question and the second is something that helps to construct a new understanding of the text. Another way of saying this is simply to say texts do not have intrinsic meanings; meaning is something made by a reader in a particular context, working with a particular materiality. In other words, there is no 'text in itself' untroubled by context and reader activity: texts are always read and understood in relation to other texts. But a context is only ever a temporary fixing of meaning, as contexts change meaning changes. However, sometimes context is used to support claims about a fixed meaning guaranteed by an authorial intention. In such arguments, the moment of production is presented as the novel's only context. Again, we see this when Claeys claims that 'unhistorical and uncontextual' readings of *Nineteen Eighty-Four* 'usually produce quite pessimistic conclusions respecting Orwell's intentions and the aims of the text' (424). Claeys seems to think that the moment of production is the only context in which one can pin down the meaning of the novel.

Lucy Sargisson also seems to think that the meaning of a text can be fixed by an author and a particular historical context. To understand utopias, she says, 'we need to understand their context. Utopias are born of discontent with the now; and, without a working knowledge of the author's and her or his contemporary reader's now, we cannot understand their dreams of a better future' (2011: 42). But this is only true if our sole purpose is to understand the original moment of production. If we want to know how Thomas More, William Morris, Ursula Le Guin, or Charlotte Perkins Gilman are read by contemporary readers, knowing about the original moment of production is of limited value. Moreover, with Gilman, we would have to decide between at least two historical contexts: the publication of *Herland* in *The Forerunner* (magazine) in 1915 and its publication in 1979 by the *Women's Press*. Many would argue that it is the second historical context that is the most significant. While understanding the moment of production is important, it does not fix the meaning of a novel. It might help establish what an author thought they were writing, or what the first readers thought they were reading, but it will contribute very little to a discussion of what a novel might mean, and the political effects it might produce, when it is read by other readers in other contexts. Angelika Bammer writes of the feminist utopias of the 1970s that 'the feminism of these texts can only be understood if it is contextualized, i.e. seen historically' (1991: 63). She then goes on to say, 'The same goes for their utopianism. In order to see, much less understand, the utopian dimension of a particular text, one must have a sense of the historical givens in opposition to which it projects an alternative' (63). While this is perfectly true if what we are trying to achieve is an understanding of a text in its specific moment of production. But if we think this is the only valid way to understand a text, we are committing a profound historical foreshortening, proposing that a text has only one historical context.

Meaning is not fixed by a historical moment of production or an authorial intention; it is made and remade in a continuous flow of historical moments of consumption. The history of a text does not end once an author stops writing or the first readers put down the book, fixing meaning forever. Consumption also has a history and, moreover, it is in this history that the ongoing meaning of the text is established. The production of meaning is not a singular event but a continuous process accompanying the historical existence of a text. It can be made to signify in many different ways in many different contexts and the process is endless in the continuing historical existence of a text. Again, *Herland* is an excellent example. The novel had very few readers when it was first published in a magazine in 1915 but following its publication in 1979 by the Women's Press it quickly became a key text in feminist utopian studies. Moreover, it remains a key academic text, one that is now compulsory reading on many university campuses. To limit it to its original moment of production is of very dubious value. We must keep in critical focus the continuing historical moments of consumption. Although never read outside a historical context, reading is not confined to the moment of the text's production. There are many other moments of consumption, with other 'historical givens', when the text is read differently because the context and political concerns have changed. While it is interesting to analyse how *News from Nowhere* or *Herland* or *The Female Man* was produced in specific historical contexts, we must remain open to the fact that the contemporary consumption of these novels takes place in very different contexts. Moreover, these contexts of consumption are just as historical as the original context of production. To think of texts historically does not mean to simply fix them 'uni-accentually' in their original moment of production. To really think historically, we must recognize that each moment of consumption, involving the making of meaning, is always itself historical. In other words, both production and consumption are historical, and if we do not recognize this, we imposed a strange kind of history on our critical analysis, one that would never allow us to fully comprehend the important struggles that occur over the meaning of texts. What is most important in political terms, therefore, is not just what a novel signified in its moment of production but what it has been made to signify in its continuing moments of consumption. It is this continuing 'multi-accentual' struggle over meaning that should be at the forefront of our critical engagement with various types of textualities (Storey, 2021a; Volosinov, 1973). Moreover, in terms of the argument made here, there is only one context for the politics of utopian fiction and that is the context in which it is read. To think this politically, what is important is not what a text means (returned to its original moment of production or to an authorial intention) but what it can be made to mean in contemporary social practices of reading.

The making of meaning is always a combination of the materiality of the text and the social practice of reading situated in a particular context. Le Guin explains it thus, 'As you read [a book] word by word and page by page, you participate in its creation, just as a cellist playing a Bach suite participates, note by note, in the creation, the coming-to-be, the existence, of the music. And, as you read and re-read, the book of course participates in the creation of you, your thoughts and feelings' (quoted in Ruppert, 1986: 146). Reading is a material activity and not the passive reception of the materiality of the text. Although it is true that readers produce meaning, they do not produce it from nothing – they are enabled and constrained by the materiality of the text. To paraphrase what Marx (1977) said about the making of history, readers make meaning, but they do not make it just as they please; they do not make it under circumstances chosen by themselves, but under circumstances directly encountered, given, and transmitted from the past, including the materiality of words on the page. Reading is a 'making' amidst the 'circumstances' of textuality and history. The relationship between reader and text is dynamic and interactive. The discourses of text and reader produce discourses that did not exist prior to acts of reading. Part of what might be new is the possibility of politics. If politics is the playing out of power, the phrase the politics of utopian fiction must refer to how reading enables the *doing* of politics, and, quite simply, it cannot *do* politics without readers. We must distinguish between politics and textual politics (see Storey, 2021b).

Utopian fiction circulates in two different economies, one concerned with exchange-value and the other focused on use-value. Both economies are important when thinking about utopian fiction, but if our critical concern is politics, then only the economy of use-value will enable us to understand what might happen politically. In the first economy, books exist as commodities to be sold to readers. In the second, there is the possibility of resistance to the commodity form: if readers buy them and then read them, we have the production of meaning and it is in the production of meaning that the possibility of politics begins to emerge. But, of course, the use-value of a commodity, even a book, cannot be known in advance of actual consumption. If meaning cannot be known prior to the social act of reading, no amount of textual analysis, regardless of how sophisticated and convincing, is able to predict how a text will be consumed and any consequences which may follow from consumption, including what we might call the politics of utopian fiction. Put simply, it is how readers read utopian fiction that makes such a politics possible. Books may not be 'silently grateful for being read' (Hudson, 2013: 16), as the narrator of *A Crystal Age* insists, but unless they are read, there can be no production of meaning, and without the production of meaning, there can be no political relations between the words of a text and the actions of a reader. There is of course no guarantee that reading will work in this way. But unless we include reading, there is absolutely no possibility of 'politics' happening at all. Therefore, to speak about the politics of utopian fiction without including the practices and outcomes of reading is to be discoursing at such a high level of abstraction as to be almost meaningless.

Unless a text is read, it is of very limited value to describe it as political. It is what a reader makes of a text that opens the very possibility of politics. How they include it in interactions with others. How they talk about it and how they use it to talk about other things. It is from this that the politics of utopian fiction may emerge. Outside of this encounter, there are no politics that can be revealed by textual analysis. It is simply not possible to know political effects in advance of the social practice of reading. Any other claim to politics is abstract and pure speculation. Put very simply, and counter to a great deal of 'common sense' in literary criticism, without a reader, such effects are not possible. The politics of utopian fiction are not in a text but in the after-effects of the experience of reading a text. It is something that requires both a text and a reader: the coming together of text and reader in an interactive and productive relationship of disturbance and defamiliarization, in which the future is imagined differently, and the present is seen no longer as inevitable but as historical and therefore changeable. The politics of utopian fiction can only ever exist in the disruptive effects they produce in the act of reading. If such reading does not bring about a break with the self-evident, the natural and the inevitable, it is difficult to know what one might mean by the politics of utopian fiction. As I have discussed elsewhere (Storey, 2021b), utopian fiction is always structured around an implicit or explicit dialogue between two communities, nowhere and the somewhere of the origin of the narration. Readers are invited to take sides in this dialogue. But unless the communities of author and reader are the same, and the passing of time will make this more and more unlikely, there will always be in fact a third community. That is, the shifting existential space of readers, and it is likely that this will eventually replace the community of the origin of the narration as the main point of contrast with nowhere. Being actively engaged in this two- and three-way conversation encourages readers to view the world around them – the third community involved in the reading of utopian fiction – as historical and therefore changeable.

Can reading initiate social practices of politics? It is a very difficult question to answer. But if we believe that politics are not simply a reflex of material circumstances and that such circumstances are mediated by the making of meaning, then why should we not consider the reading of utopian fiction as one possible source for political action? To dream politically is not some hopeless mode of escapism, it is a challenge to complacency and complicity. It can challenge the idea that the here and now is the inevitable result of the human condition. Hope loosens us from the hold of the present. John Macquarrie, a conservative Christian, an idea that would have puzzled the religion's founder and his original followers, worries about the future-focus of hope, concerned that it might encourage 'unrealistic and utopian hopes' (quoted in Eagleton, 2017: 69). But, as I have argued elsewhere, because what we call reality is not inevitable (Storey, 2019), defining it is fundamental to the workings of hegemony. Probably, the most famous example of utopian graffiti was written on a wall in Paris in May 1968. It read 'Soyez Realistes, Demandez L'impossible' (be realistic, demand the impossible). What it suggests is that reality structures and mediates our experience of the real. It also suggests that being realistic in a traditional way can make us complicit with a reality which is only ever a version constructed in the interest of those with power. Therefore, to escape an oppressive construction of reality, we must be realistic in a different way and demand what that oppressive reality insists is impossible and in so doing break our complicity with it. If much of what we do and think is shaped by habit, reading utopian fiction can challenge us to take seriously the promise of possibility. It can provide us with a language of hope which can in turn enable us to articulate a desire for a future better than the present. Without hope, it is hard to act at all. Hope is the feeling that something is possible. But I do not mean optimism as some facile view that things will always get better, but militant optimism as a force to keep alive the hope that they can be *made* better by collective human action.

But we should not expect too much from utopian fiction. It has a part to play in politics, but it cannot be political on its own. Without readers, it cannot be much at all. Books on shelves do not make revolutions; people do, and for some people, it is reading which brings them into the struggle. Diane Griffin Crowder's account of reading utopian fiction in the 1970s provides some evidence of how it might work:

> I bought and read all the utopian works I could get my hands on, and I felt a powerful emotional response to most of them. These novels gave me a fictional representation of the unexpressed anger I felt at abuses I saw daily but felt powerless to stop .... I could for a few hours imagine myself in these utopian worlds and come away with a modicum of hope that, despite the depressing evidence of my daily newspapers, we could in fact make a better world'.

> (quoted in Beaumont, 2009: 87)

Matthew Beaumont dismisses this as an example of what he calls 'individual consciousness', claiming that 'Utopian fiction necessarily remains anchored to the room in which it is written and read'

(Beaumont, 2009: 89). But why should this be the case. If this were true what is the point of Marx and Engels writing the *Communist Manifesto*? If we think 'material conditions' can by themselves produce social change, then utopianism is little more than fantasy escapism. But this is a version of 'materialism' that predates Marx; it is certainly not 'historical'.[5] As Gramsci contends, 'It may be ruled out that immediate economic crises of themselves produce fundamental historical events; they can simply create a terrain more favourable to the dissemination of certain modes of thought, and certain ways of posing and resolving questions involving the entire subsequent development of national life' (1971: 184). Material conditions do not dictate the terms of change, social change is always driven by both objective and subjective factors; therefore culture, including utopianism, is politically important. Crowder's is only one account, but it is indicative of how reading utopian fiction might work politically. Moreover, we should not discard the significance of her final words, an after-effect of her reading, 'we could in fact make a better world'.

When interviewed on the UK's *Channel Four News* (15.10.19), after jointly winning the Booker Prize for Fiction for *The Testaments*, the sequel to *The Handmaid's Tale*, Margaret Atwood said this of dystopian fiction: 'There are a lot of possible futures .... What dystopian novels about the future do is say here is a blueprint for a house. Is this where you would like to live? Is this the world you would like to live in? If you would not like to live in this world, take a different road'. Many readers of *The Handmaid's Tale* have started to walk that road.[6] On 21 January 2017, the day after Donald Trump's presidential inauguration, the Women's March took place in Washington, DC. Many women on the march made visible reference to the novel. It took two particular forms: women dressed as handmaids of Gilead and women carrying placards with variations on the message, 'The Handmaid's Tale is not an instruction manual'. Since the march, women dressed as handmaids have become something of an international sign of protest, especially when the issue is reproductive rights and abortion. In this way, and in a particular version of the *Ozymandias effect* (see Storey, 2021b), what is dystopian is made radically utopian as women dressed as handmaids perform a double articulation: pointing to an imaginary future to reveal things about the problems of the present, and in the gap that opens between what is and what could be, they begin, through acts of consumption, to defamiliarize the manufactured naturalness and the hopeless inevitability of the here and now, making it conceivable to believe that another world is possible.

NOTES

1 Williams, sharing many of the concerns discussed in Chapter 6, also writes of 'the reproduction of a restricted everyday reality' (2010: 175) and 'the pressure of habitual forms and ideas' (1965: 10) and explains that 'all of us, as individuals, grow up within a society, within the rules of a society, and these rules cut very deep, and include certain ways of seeing the world, certain ways of talking about the world. All the time people are being born into a society, shown what to see, shown how to talk about it' (1989: 21–22).

2 For example, being objectively oppressed is rarely enough to produce resistance, we must recognize our subordination as oppression.

3 Hoggart's book is divided into two distinct parts. Unfortunately, the second part drifts unhelpfully towards what the first part seeks to challenge.

4 Of course, the first reader of a text is always its author. As most authors know, it is only when they read what they have written that they begin to get a sense of what it means. A text emerges not just from writing but from a continual process of reading and rereading.

5 Once historical is added to materialism, it changes materialism from something fixed and expressive to something that is open to change and articulation.

6 Contrary to what Atwood suggests, utopian fiction is not political because of the solutions it points to in the future ('blueprints') but because of the problems it allows readers to identify in the present ('radical utopianism').

POSTSCRIPT

ANTI-CONSUMPTION

As I hope has been demonstrated throughout the proceeding seven chapters, consumption is an important and complex sociological concept. It points to what people do, what capitalism needs them to do, and to a way of thinking critically about human agency, use and meaning. There are many things we have not discussed in this short book, but with the space remaining, I will briefly outline four examples of the discourse of anti-consumption.[1] The first challenge is organized around the idea that consumption is a pathology, the second advocates a return to 'simplicity', and the third and fourth, the most obviously 'political', seek to organize opposition to consumerism.

The word affluenza combines affluence and influenza to suggest that consumerism is a kind of pathology, a condition of individuals, who, while struggling to 'keep up with the Joneses', fall deeper and deeper into unhappiness (Hamilton and Dennis, 2005; James, 2007). While 'Happiness' studies (see Layard, 2011) are right to point to the fact that quality of life is not something that can only be achieved through consumption, and that retail therapy may not be therapy at all, to casually suggest that individual consumption is the problem and that stopping consuming so much will make us happier is to sidestep questions of inequality and power.[2] It is all very well to say stop buying things and instead take a walk on the beach or an evening with friends, as if these did not involve consumption, including transport, clothing, food, and drink, and that these 'simple' activities are themselves governed by inequality and power. If consumerism was driven by an inherent acquisitive impulse – people are just

DOI: 10.4324/9781003224471-8

naturally greedy – why has this only manifested itself under the capitalist mode of production? While it is true that people have always consumed, it is not true that there has always been consumerism. Therefore, consumerism cannot be explained by focusing on individual greed and an explanation should be sought elsewhere. A start would be to give it its correct name, capitalist consumerism.

The Voluntary Simplicity Movement advocates a reduction in consumption as part of a broader strategy that claims 'we can work less, want less, and spend less, and be happier in the process' (Linda Breen Pierce; quoted in Maniates, 2002: 199). What is called for goes under different names: downshifting, downsizing, or simply simplifying. As Michael Maniates asks, is it 'a subversive attempt to strike at the heart of consumer capitalism? Or is it an irrelevant subculture, one that has enjoyed more than its share of media attention?' (2002: 202). While it is possible to point to how we seem to have chosen more spending power rather than a reduction in working hours, we must be careful about who is included within the parameters of the pronoun. Put simply, the decision about reducing hours versus consuming less was not one in which most people had a say. Unless buying less is matched by working less, a reduction in consumption would mean an increase in unemployment. These are not individual choices but matters that demand massive and fundamental structural change.

Simple living and downshifting tend to be a practice pursued by the affluent. As Jo Littler points out, 'One problem of the practice of deliberately consuming less is that it is by definition an option practiced by those with enough resources and cultural capital to be able to consume in the first place. The poor may be under-consumers, but this is rarely by active choice' (2009: 107). Maniates cites an example of 12 ways we can simplify how we live:

1. Avoid shopping, 2. Leave the car parked, 3. Live in a nice neighbourhood (that will allow you to walk to stores or easily access public transport), 4. Get rid of your lawn, 5. Cut down on your laundry, 6. Block junk mail, 7. Turn off the TV, 8. Communicate by email, 9. Don't use a cellular phone, 10. Drink water rather than store-bought beverages, 11. Patronize your public library, and 12. Limit the size of your family.

(quoted in Maniates, 2002: 211)

Leaving to one side how offensively inappropriate this advice is to the billions of people around the world who involuntarily under-consume, its many assumptions, especially around social class, make it also deeply problematic in the affluent west. Can everyone simply choose to live in a nice neighbourhood?

The *Adbusters Media Foundation*, a Canadian-based, but globally active, anti-consumerism group founded by Kalle Lasn in 1989, see themselves as revolutionaries fighting 'a guerrilla information war fought not in the sky or on the streets ... but in newspapers and magazines, on radio, TV and in cyberspace' (quoted in Bordwell, 2002: 250).[3] The main weapon in this war is the practice of 'culture jamming'. Tim Jordan defines this as 'an attempt to reverse and transgress the meaning of the cultural codes whose primary aim is to persuade us to buy something or be someone' (2002: 102). Its aim is to free human consciousness from the fantasy world of capitalist consumerism. As Rick Poyner argues, 'Advertising's right to colonise the physical environment of the street and act as primary shaper of the mental environment is taken for granted and there is no officially sanctioned public competition for the thoughts, beliefs, imagination and desires of the passer-by. Apart from other ads' (quoted in Bordwell, 2002: 238).

The *Foundation* publishes a magazine, *Adbusters*, runs a website, organizes events, such as the *No Shopping Day*, *TV Turn-Off Week*, *World Car-Free Day*, *Buy-Nothing Christmas*, and produces what it calls 'subvertisements' and 'uncommercials'.

> I quite openly say that the bulk of us are caught in a media-consumer trance; that we basically sit down in front of the TV sets every night and absorb consumption messages ... And then on Saturday mornings we hop into our cars and dash off to the malls and do exactly what all those ads have been telling us to do. I think most of us are living lives of mindless consumption. I think we are dupes.
>
> (Kalle Lasn, interviewed by Kim Humphrey in 2006; quoted in Humphrey, 2010: 89; see also Lasn, 1999)[4]

Although Lasn is careful to use the pronoun 'we', it is quite clear that he does not really include himself in its collectivity – people 'living lives of mindless consumption'. Rather than go down to the mall zombie-like and buy what he has been told to buy, he organizes No Shopping Days and produces 'subvertisements' and 'uncommericials' (see Lasn, 1999). This is vanguard politics of an enlightened few struggling amid a manipulated many.

In a lot of anti-consumption rhetoric what should be a critique of capitalist consumerism often gets lost in a moral argument about individual consumption. To blame the individual consumer for confusing genuine needs with frivolous desires is to fall for the neoliberal fantasy that the sovereign consumer drives economic life. In such a critique, capitalism is guilty of nothing more than trying to keep up with demand. But before we define capitalist consumerism as a moral problem, and begin to blame consumers for its existence, we should remind ourselves that consumption is fundamental to capitalism. Many positions of anti-consumption tend to ignore the fact that capitalism depends on consumption. Without it, production would cease and with it the flow of profits. Consumerism is the ideology of this need.[5] While capitalism's ever-increasing demand for growth is a problem, to blame this on individual consumers is at best an act of political displacement, producing analysis that is both naïve and complicit with power. Too often it amounts to little more than moralism underpinned by dubious psychology and a solution that is hopelessly fixated on little more than various versions of self-help.

While it is true that consumption generally needs to stay within sustainable limits to reduce pressure on the planet and its resources, we should not lose sight of the fact that incredible levels of inequality mark contemporary consumption. Put simply, the rich need to consume less and the poor consume more. This might be possible in a reformed capitalism. Although it is difficult to be precise, Maniates estimates that about one billion people over-consume and four billion do not consume enough (2002: 206). It is estimated that the richest 20 per cent of the world's population are responsible for about 85 per cent of total private spending (Humphrey, 2010: 6). Such figures are hardly surprising when we place them together with the massively unequal global distribution of wealth. It is estimated that 62 richest people in the world own as much as the poorest 3.6 billion and the richest 1% (about 73 million) own as much as everyone else put together (7.3 billion).[6] To simply moralize about sustainability and individual consumption and ignore the massive inequalities of consumption is to promote a politics that capitalism is very willing to support. Moralism tends to condemn from a lofty position of absolute certainty. Of course, no such position ever really exists.

As I hope is evident from what has been discussed so far, none of these forms of anti-consumption take us beyond consumption as a key sociological concept or the theoretical frames we have discussed to explain consumption as a social practice. One final example should make this very clear, Laura Portman-Stacer's excellent account of the anti-consumption patterns of a group of American anarchists. As with any social identity, anarchism is supported by forms of consumption, constructing what it means to assume a politicized identity. Like consumption, anti-consumption is both material and discursive, a doing and the articulation of what is done. Although it represents a rejection of what is regarded as mainstream consumption, it is not a lifestyle without consumption. Therefore, we should not think of anti-consumption as a rejection of consumption. As we noted in Chapter 2, this would be impossible. While it is true, that the anarchists she interviews are trying to find 'alternatives to capitalist exchange' (2012: 93), this does not mean they are not consuming. What they are doing is trying to find alternatives to what they think of as mainstream consumption. So, for example, while the car is rejected, public transport and cycling are consumed as alternative modes of transport. It is through this combination of rejection and alternatives that anarchism as a mode of consumption becomes visible to itself and mainstream society. The selective consumption has at least three aims: denying money to capitalism, a system they wish to destroy; articulating a sense of identity and solidarity with those with whom they share a politics; performing a prefigurative politics in a theatrical display of an alternative to capitalism.

Working with a distinction, we encountered in Chapter 3, between 'needs' and 'wants', consumption is sorted by Portman-Stacer's anarchists into two categories, things to be avoided and things that confirm an anti-capitalist identity. However, what she calls 'conspicuous anti-consumption' (99) could just as accurately be called, using terms discussed earlier, 'conspicuous consumption' or the making of 'social distinction' and 'cultural capital' or 'secondary production' or 'performativity'. Therefore, what appears to be the opposite of consumption is in fact better understood as a very particular form of consumption, which can be examined using the same theories explained earlier to explore more mainstream forms of consumption.

For the anarchists she interviewed, 'needs are distinguished from luxuries through a critical lens that understands most consumer desires to be the product of false consciousness, induced by corporations, in the interest of promoting rampant material acquisition' (90). But is false consciousness a useful way to think about consumption? Marx points to the fact that the expansion of consumption is contradictory. On the one hand, it helps reproduce capitalism, while, on the other, it increases the desire of workers to expect more. It was these increasing expectations that produced what he called a 'civilizing moment' (1973: 287). To consume, the worker needs wages; to consume more, he or she needs higher wages. In this way, then, the stimulation of the expansion of consumer desire both stabilizes and threatens the foundations of the system. That is, by producing ever more needs and promoting ever more desires, the system 'educates' consumers to demand even more with the possible effect that demand may exceed what capitalism is able to produce. In other words, capitalism may encourage the desire to consume to a point beyond which it cannot deliver on its promises: at this moment, the system is potentially confronted by its 'gravediggers' (Marx and Engels, 1998: 24). It is now a question of which comes first, the revolutionary work of gravediggers or capitalism's successful attempt to turn the planet into a graveyard. Do we bury the system or does the system bury us?

Like all books, this one is unfinished. It is now up to readers, in their own processes of consumption, to take what they have gathered here and carry it into their own productions, whether written or spoken, and begin the ever-ongoing work of completion.

NOTES

1 Consumerism is not without its ethical alternatives: fair trade, recycling, consumer boycotts, green shopping, and buycotts. For an excellent account of ethical consumption, see Littler (2016). Two very interesting

accounts of anti-consumption can be found in Humphrey (2010) and Littler (2009).

2 As Kim Humphrey points out, 'Measured levels of subjective wellbeing in western countries do not rise with income, but nor do they significantly fall; they tend to remain fairly constant over time, and this constant is relatively high. Moreover, in international terms, wealthy nations tend consistently to exhibit high national average levels of subjective wellbeing relative to other countries' (2010: 146).

3 Find out more at https://www.adbusters.org/about-us.

4 See also the excellent interview with Jo Littler (http://www.signsofthe times.org.uk/The_shoe.html).

5 On the Adbusters website, you will find a t-shirt, parodying the iconic First World War recruitment poster, with the slogan *Your Economy Needs You to Consume*.

6 Figures quoted in the *i* newspaper (18/1/16).

GLOSSARY

Active and passive audience   This is a distinction found in discussions of media consumption. An active audience is said to make meaning from what it consumes, while a passive audience, it is claimed, simply accepts the meaning intended.

Affluenza   A portmanteau word, combining affluence and influenza, to suggest that mass consumption is a kind of pathology.

Agency   The term is usually used in conjunction with *structure* to denote a relationship between what we can do and the constraints on our activities.

Alienation   Used by Karl Marx to describe the loss of creativity and control experienced by workers under the capitalist *mode of production*.

Anthropocene   The name given to the claim that we now live in the 'age of humans', pointing to our impact on the planet that can be readily seen in the geological record. The inclusion of all humankind as responsible is challenged by the concept of the *Capitalocene.*

Anti-consumption   This is best understood as a form of alternative or selective consumption rather than the absence of consumption.

Capitalism   The dominant economic system throughout the world, including versions of state capitalism. It has been developing and increasing its power for about 500 years.

Capitalocene   This is an alternative name for the *Anthropocene.* Its use is a rejection of the false universalism of the claim that all humans are equally culpable for the climate crisis. Instead, it points to capitalism as responsible for the negative impact on the planet.

Class struggle Although Karl Marx did not invent the idea of social class, he did more than most to suggest that societies are shaped by an underlying conflict between social classes, especially the determination of the dominant class to remain the ruling class.

Commodity An item produced for sale within the capitalist system.

Commodity fetishism A concept developed by Karl Marx to describe how the products of capitalism appear in the marketplace for sale as if by magic, concealing the conditions of the labour that produced them.

Common sense This is not another term for good sense. According to Antonio Gramsci, it is the kind of thinking and consequent actions that support the *hegemony* of the dominant class.

Concept A formulation intended to explain something. It can be concrete or abstract. We use concepts to understand and communicate our understanding of the world.

Conspicuous consumption A term coined by Thorstein Veblen to describe the *consumption* practices of a new 'leisure class' that developed in the USA at the close of the nineteenth century.

Consumer capitalism A stage in the development of capitalism that begins to become visible towards the end of the seventeenth century.

Consumption This can mean at least two things. First, the acquisition and use of something. Second, an account of acquisition and use, which stresses the role played by human *agency*.

Context A context consists of the texts we introduce to understand something. These other texts help to partially fix meaning. If, during a conversation, you use the word 'it', your meaning will only become clear if you provide a context that indicates to what 'it' refers. However, we should not think of contexts as only texts being joined with other texts. When we try to make sense of a **text**, we always bring to it a set of presuppositions which provide a framework for our analysis. These assumptions help construct a specific context for our understanding of the text – these are woven together around the text to be analysed. The use of a theoretical perspective is the most obvious example of this second aspect of context.

Cultural capital A social currency based on knowledge, familiarity, and the ability to feel at ease with the texts and practices of 'high' culture. It derives from the work of Pierre Bourdieu.

Cultural jamming In relation to consumption, it is the practice of subverting advertising, and the **culture** around advertising, to challenge the taken-for-grantedness of capitalist consumerism.

Cultural studies The name of an academic approach to culture, first developed in the 1960s at the Centre for Contemporary Cultural Studies, University of Birmingham, UK.

Culture Raymond Williams claims that culture is one of the most complicated words in the English language. Here it is used in two ways. First, to point to a particular way of life. Second, as a realized signifying system, as developed in *cultural studies* by, and in work influenced by, Williams.

Culture Industry This is a term developed by the *Frankfurt School* to describe the supposed homogeneity and predictability of the cultural output of institutions like Hollywood, mass publishing, and television.

Discourse A concept developed by Michel Foucault. He argues that discourses enable, constrain, and constitute our understanding of things. Discourses can be grouped together in what he calls a discursive formation. There are other understandings of discourse, but they do not appear in this book.

Ethnography The study of the *culture* of a group or a people from the perspective of what it is they do. It usually involves participant observation.

Everyday life This refers to all those aspects of ordinary social existence which seem to go unnoticed beneath the veil of habit and routine. It has been a key focus of much sociology.

False consciousness It is said to exist when what a person thinks and how they act does not appear to correspond to their objective circumstances.

Frankfurt School It is the name given to a group of German intellectuals associated with the Institute for Social research at the University of Frankfurt. Their work is often a combination of **Marxism** and **Freudianism**. Following the coming to power of Nazism in Germany in 1933, the Institute moved to New York. The experience of life in the USA had a profound impact on their work on consumption.

Freudianism Refers to a body of work – psychoanalysis – developed by Sigmund Freud and his followers. It seeks to discover the unconscious motivations in *everyday life*.

Globalization The development of a global market for capitalist commodities. It begins to appear in the late eighteenth century, accelerating in the 1990s.

Hedonism The seeking of pleasure and the belief that pleasure is the ultimate human motivation.

Hegemony A concept developed by Antonio Gramsci to describe how class rule is based on the building of consensus rather than straightforward coercion. However, it is worth remembering that, for Gramsci, if not for everyone who uses the concept, consensus is always underpinned by the threat of coercion.

Homo economicus The rational and self-interested subject at the centre of much mainstream economics.

Homologies Refers to things that have a similar relation, function, or structure.

Identity Our sense of who we are and who we would like to be to other people. Consumption plays a significant role in the construction of identities.

Leavisism The name given to FR Leavis and his followers, Leavisites, who, at their peak between the 1930s and 1950s, argued that *mass culture* was becoming a threat to *culture*.

Lysergic acid diethylamide (LSD) The hallucinogenic drug synthesized by the Swiss chemist Albert Hoffmann in 1938 (although he did not become aware of its effects until 1943). It has been used in psychology, for military purposes, and was the central drug of the counterculture of the 1960s.

Manipulation The action of changing or influencing how we behave, usually for the benefit of those doing the manipulating.

Mass consumption As with *mass culture*, the term mass is not innocently descriptive. While it can signify the *consumption* practices of the many, more often it indicates a judgement about lack of taste and inferior goods.

Mass culture As with *mass consumption*, the term mass is not innocently descriptive. While it can signify the *culture* of the many, more often it indicates a judgement about its inferiority.

Masses A term used for the working class. Sometimes a descriptive ascription, but more often a judgement on the class's supposed homogeneity. Raymond Williams famously said, an opinion I share, that there are no masses, only ways of seeing other people as masses.

Marxism A theory and politics derived from the work of Karl Marx. When used to describe sociological work, it usually indicates an insistence on the importance of considering history and power, especially in terms of class relations.

Mediatization A concept developed to explore and explain how media have become increasingly significant in *everyday life*.

Mode of production A concept developed by Karl Marx to explain how at different times in history, humans have organized production in a variety of distinctive ways. Key modes of production include slave, feudal, and capitalist.

Multi-accentuality A concept developed by Russian theorist Valentin Volosinov. It seeks to explore how we can make many meanings of the same thing. This is not because the thing is rich in meaning but because of what we bring to it. Uni-accentuality is the attempt to fix meaning as singular. It is a strategy often used by those with power.

Object determinism The view that the value and meaning of something is inherent in the thing itself.

Ozymandias effect A concept developed by John Storey to explore how dystopian fiction often includes a utopian conclusion.

Parapraxis Better known as a 'Freudian slip'. It is used by Sigmund Freud to explain how we often say or do things, which we say we did not intend, but which on analysis reveal a great deal about our unconscious motivations.

Performativity A concept developed by Judith Butler to explain the cultural constructedness of sex and gender. It has its origins in JL Austin's work on language and Jacques Derrida's critique of this work.

Postmodernism Usually refers to two possibilities: the collapse of meta-narratives that claim to have a unique access to the truth of things and the weakening of the distinction between high and popular culture, first noticed in the 1960s.

Practice A term for human action that can be found in a variety of sociological and philosophical traditions. A practice consists of an interconnected series of both physical and mental activities, in which bodily actions (ways of doing something) are combined with mental actions (modes of interpretation, learned assumptions, presuppositions, and expectations).

Regime of truth A concept developed by Michel Foucault. He argues that all societies organize themselves around truths that are not necessarily true but are acted on as if they are true.

Romantic ethic An idea developed by Colin Campbell to explore the connection between Romanticism, the cultural movement which developed across Europe alongside industrialization in the late eighteenth century, and the establishment of *mass consumption*.

Secondary production A term coined by Michel de Certeau to point to the ways in which *consumption* is an active process and not something determined by production.

Social distinction Pierre Bourdieu uses the term to identify how *consumption* is used to make, mark, and maintain social difference, especially to support and reproduce class inequalities.

Social emulation A once popular way of explaining *consumption*, arguing that modes of consuming flow emulatory from the top to the bottom of societies.

Structure Usually used in conjunction with *agency* to denote a relationship between human action and what constrains it.

Sustainable consumption This refers to *consumption* that does not threaten the life of the planet.

Text A text does have to be something written; it can be anything that can be made to carry meaning.

Theory A systematic combination of concepts that are grouped together to explain something.

Use-value, exchange-value, and value Concepts that derive from the work of Karl Marx. The first two seek to draw attention to how commodities exist in two economies, of sale and of use, and that there is no necessary determining relationship between the two. Value is the human labour materialized in the thing produced.

Utopian fiction Novels and short stories that depict an imagined future in the hope of challenging the taken-for-grantedness of the here and now.

REFERENCES

Abrams, MH. 1953. *The Mirror and the Lamp: Romantic Theory and the Critical Tradition*, New York: Oxford University Press.

Adorno, TW. 1991. In JM Bernstein (ed. with intro), *The Cultural Industry: Selected Essays on Mass Culture*, London: Routledge.

Adorno, TW. and Horkheimer, M. 1979. *Dialectic of Enlightenment*, London: Verso.

Althusser, L. 2019. 'Ideology and Ideological State Apparatuses'. In J. Storey (ed.), *Cultural Theory and Popular Culture: A Reader*, 5th edition, London: Routledge, 403–413.

Austin, JL. 1962. *How to Do Things with Words*, Oxford: Clarendon Press.

Bammer, A. 1991. *Partial Visions*, London: Routledge.

Beaumont, M. 2009. *Utopia Ltd*, Chicago, IL: Haymarket Books.

Berger, P. and Luckmann, T. 1991. *The Social Construction of Reality*, Harmondsworth: Penguin.

Bermingham, A. 1995. 'The Consumption of Culture: Image, Object, Text'. In A Bermingham and J Brewer (eds.), *The Consumption of Culture 1600-1800: Image, Object, Text*, London: Routledge, 1–20.

Blumer, H. 1969. *Symbolic Interactionism: Perspective and Method*, Englewood Cliffs, NJ: Prentice-Hall.

Bonneuil, C. and Fressoz, J-B. 2017. *The Shock of the Anthropocene*, London: Verso.

Bordwell, M. 2002. 'Jamming Culture: Adbusters' Hip Media Campaign against Consumerism'. In T Princen, M Maniates and K Conca (eds.), *Confronting Consumption*, Cambridge, MA: MIT Press, 237–253.

Bould, M. 2021. *The Anthropocene Unconscious*, London: Verso.

Bourdieu, P. 1992. *Distinction: A Social Critique of the Judgement of Taste*, London: Routledge.

Bowlby, R. 1985. *Just Looking*, London: Methuen.

Brecht, B. 1978. *On Theatre*, London: Methuen.

Brecht, B. 1980. 'Against Georg Lukacs'. In New Left Review (ed.), *Aesthetics and Politics*, London: Verso, 68–85.

Butler, J. 1993. *Bodies that Matter*, New York: Routledge.

Butler, J. 1999. *Gender Trouble*, New York: Routledge.

Campbell, C. 1983. 'Romanticism and the Consumer Ethic: Intimations of a Weber-Style Thesis', *Sociological Analysis*, 44:4, 279–295.

Campbell, C. 1987. *The Romantic Ethic and the Spirit of Modern Consumerism*, Oxford: Basil Blackwell.

Campbell, C. 1993. 'Understanding Traditional and Modern Patterns of Consumption in Eighteenth-Century England: A Character-Action Approach'. In J Brewer and R Porter (eds.), *Consumption and the World of Goods*, London: Routledge, 40–57.

Chinn, S. 1997. 'Gender Performativity'. In A Medhurst and SR Munt (eds.), *The Lesbian and Gay Studies Reader*, London: Cassell, 293–301.

Claeys, G. 2018. *Dystopia*, Oxford: Oxford University Press.

Corrigan, P. 1997. *The Sociology of Consumption*, London: Sage Publications.

de Beauvoir, S. 1984. *The Second Sex*, New York: Vintage.

de Certeau, M. 1984. *The Practice of Everyday Life*. Berkeley, CA: University of California Press.

de Certeau, M. 2019. 'The Practice of Everyday Life'. In J. Storey (ed.), *Cultural Theory and Popular Culture: A Reader*, 5th edition, London: Routledge, 601–611.

Derrida, J. 1982. *Margins of Philosophy*, Chicago, IL: University of Chicago Press.

Douglas, M. and Isherwood, B. 1996. *The World of Goods: Towards an Anthropology of Consumption*, London: Routledge.

Eagleton, T. 2017. *Hope without Optimism*, New Haven, CT and London: Yale University Press.

Eco, U. 1985. 'Reflections on "The Name of the Rose"', *Encounter*, 64:4, 7–19.

Ellis, EC. 2018. *Anthropocene*, Oxford: Oxford University Press.

Ewen, S. 1976. *Captains of Consciousness: Advertising and the Social Roots of the Conscious Society*, New York: McGraw-Hill.

Ewen, S. and Ewen, E. 1982. *Channels of Desire*, New York: McGraw-Hill.

Fine, B. and Leopold, E. 1990. 'Consumerism and the Industrial Revolution', *Social History*, 15:2, 151–179.

Foucault, M. 1981. *The History of Sexuality. Volume One: An Introduction*, trans. R. Hurley, Harmondsworth: Penguin.

Foucault, M. 1989. *The Archaeology of Knowledge*, London: Routledge.

Foucault, M. 1991. *Discipline and Punish*, London: Penguin.

Foucault, M. 2002. *Michel Foucault Essential Works, Power*, Harmondsworth: Penguin.

Freud, S. 1973. *New Introductory Lectures*, Harmondsworth: Penguin.

Garfinkel, H. 1967. *Studies in Ethnomethodology*, Englewood Cliffs, NJ: Prentice-Hall.

Giddens, A. 1984. *The Constitution of Society*, Cambridge: Polity.

Giddens, A. 1992. *The Transformation of Intimacy*, Cambridge: Polity.

Glennie, P. 1995. 'Consumption within Historical Studies'. In D Miller (ed.), *Acknowledging Consumption*, London: Routledge, 164–203.

Goffman, E. 1990. *The Presentation of Self in Everyday Life*, London: Penguin.

Gramsci, A. 1971. *Selections from Prison Notebooks*, London: Lawrence & Wishart.

Gramsci, A. 2007. *Prison Notebooks, Volume III*, New York: Columbia University Press.

Gramsci, A. 2019. 'Hegemony, Intellectuals and the State'. In J Storey (ed.), *Cultural Theory and Popular Culture: A Reader*, 5th edition, London: Routledge, 69–74.

Green, M. 1996. 'Centre for Contemporary Cultural Studies'. In J Storey (ed.), *What Is Cultural Studies? A Reader*, London: Edward Arnold, 49–60.

Halkier, B. 2019. 'Methods and methods' debates within consumption research'. In M Keller et al. (eds.), *Routledge Handbook on Consumption*, London: Routledge, 36–46.

Hall, S. 1996a. 'Introduction: Who Needs "Identity"'. In S Hall and P du Gay (eds.), *Questions of Cultural Identity*, London: Sage, 1–17.

Hall, S. 1996b. 'When Was 'the Post-colonial'? Thinking at the Limit'. In L Chambers and L Curti (eds.), *The Post-Colonial Question*, London: Routledge, 242–260.

Hall, S. 1997. 'Introduction'. In S Hall (ed.), *Representation*, London: Sage, 1–11.

Hall, S. 2019. 'The Rediscovery of Ideology'. In J Storey (ed.), *Cultural Theory and Popular Culture: A Reader*, 5th edition, London: Routledge, 94–123.

Hamilton, C. and Denniss, R. 2005. *Affluenza: When Too Much Is Never Enough*, Sydney: Allen & Unwin.

Harvey, D. 2010. *A Companion to Marx's Capital*, London: Verso.

Hepp, A. 2013. *Cultures of Mediatization*, Cambridge: Polity.

Hjarvard, S. 2013. *The Mediatization of Culture and Society*, London: Routledge.

Hoggart, R. 1970. *Speaking to Each Other*, London: Chatto & Windus.

Hoggart, R. 1990. *The Uses of Literacy*, Harmondsworth: Penguin.

Hoggard, R. 1991. *A Sort of Clowning*, Oxford: Oxford University Press.

Horton, D. 2003. 'Green Distinctions: The Performance of Identity among Environmental Activists', *The Sociological Review*, 51:2, 63–77.

Hudson, WH. 2013. *A Crystal Age*, Create Space Independent Publishing Platform.

Hudson, I. and Hudson, M. 2021. *Consumption*, Cambridge: Polity.

Humphrey, K. 2010. *Excess: Anti-Consumerism in the West*, Cambridge: Polity.

Jackson, T. 2017. *Prosperity without Growth*, 2nd edition, London: Routledge.

James, O. 2007. *Affluenza: How to Be Successful and Stay Sane*, London: Vermilion.

Jameson, F. 1981. *The Political Unconscious*, London: Methuen.

Jameson, F. 1984. 'Postmodernism, or the Cultural Logic of Late Capitalism', *New Left Review* 165, 53–92.

Jordan, T. 2002. *Activism!: Direct Action, Hacktivism and the Future of Society*, London: Reaction Books.

Kallis, G., Paulson, S., D'Alisa, G. and Demaria, F. 2020. *The Case for Degrowth*, Cambridge: Polity.

Kernaghan, C. 1997. 'An Appeal to Walt Disney'. In A Ross (ed.), *No Sweat*, New York: Verso, 3–29.

Klein, N. 2015. *This Changes Everything*, London: Penguin.

Laclau, E. and Mouffe, C. 2001. *Hegemony and Socialist Strategy*, 2nd edition, London: Verso.

Laclau, E. and Mouffe, C. 2019. 'Post-Marxism without Apologies'. In J Storey (ed.), *Cultural Theory and Popular Culture: A Reader*, 5th edition, London: Routledge, 124–149.

Laermans, R. 1993. 'Learning to Consume: Early Department Stores and the Shaping of the Modern Consumer Culture (1860-1914)'. *Theory, Culture & Society* 10, 79–102.

Lasn, K. 1999. *Culture Jam*, New York: Eagle Books.

Latour, B. 1999. 'On Recalling ANT'. In J Law and J Hassard (eds.), *Actor Network Theory and after*, London; Oxford: Blackwell, 15–25.

Latour, B. 2007. *Reassembling the Social*, Oxford: Oxford University Press.

Layard, R. 2011. *Happiness*, Harmondsworth: Penguin.

Leary, T. 1973. *The Politics of Ecstasy*, St Albans: Paladin.

Lefebvre, H. 2002. *Critique of Everyday Life*, volume 2, London: Verso.

Levitas, R. 2014. 'We Argue How Else'. In T Moylan (ed.), *Demand the Impossible*, Bern: Peter Lang, 257–262.

Lewis, J. 2013. *Beyond Consumer Capitalism*, Cambridge: Polity.

Littler, J. 2009. *Radical Consumption: Shopping for Change in Contemporary Culture*, Maidenhead: Open University Press.

Littler, J. 2016. 'Cultural Studies and Consumer Culture'. In D Shaw et al. (eds.), *Ethics and Morality in Consumption*, London: Routledge, 233–247.

Lovell, T. 2019. 'Cultural Production'. In J Storey (ed.), *Cultural Theory and Popular Culture: A Reader*, 5th edition, London: Routledge, 595–600.

Lowenthal, L. 1961. *Literature, Popular Culture and Society*, Palo Alto: Pacific.

Mann, ME. 2021. *The New Climate War*, London: Scribe.

McBrien, J. 2016. 'Accumulating Extinction'. In JW Moore (ed.), *Anthropocene or Capitalocene?* Oakland, CA: Kairos, 116–137.

McKendrick, N. 1974. 'Home Demand and Economic Growth: A New View of the Role of Women and Children in the Industrial Revolution'. In N McKendrick (ed.), *Historical Perspectives: Studies in English Thought and Society in Honour of J. H. Plumb*, London: Europa Publications, 152–210.

McKendrick, N. 1982. 'Commercialization and the Economy'. In N McKendrick, J Brewer and JH Plumb (eds.), *The Birth of a Consumer Society*, London: Europa Publications, 9–19.

McKendrick, N., Brewer, J. and Plumb, JH. 1982. *The Birth of a Consumer Society*, London: Europa Publications.

Maniates, M. 2002. 'In Search of Consumptive Resistance: The Voluntary Simplicity Movement'. In T Princen, M Maniates and K Conca (eds.), *Confronting Consumption*, Cambridge, MA: MIT Press, 199–235.

Marcus, GE. and Fischer, MJ. 1986. *Anthropology as Cultural Critique: An Experimental Moment in the Human Sciences*, Chicago, IL: University of Chicago Press.

Marcuse, H. 2002. *One-Dimensional Man*, London: Routledge.

Marx, K. 1963. *Selected Writings in Sociology and Social Philosophy*, Harmondsworth: Penguin.

Marx, K. 1973. *Grundrisse*, Harmondsworth: Penguin.

Marx, K. 1976a. *Capital*, volume I, Harmondsworth: Penguin.

Marx, K. 1976b. *'Preface' and 'Introduction' to Contribution to a Critique of Political Economy*, Beijing: Peking Foreign Languages Press.

Marx, K. 1977. *The Eighteenth Brumaire of Louis Bonaparte*, Moscow: Progress Publishers.

Marx, K. 1992. *Early Writings*, London: Penguin.

Marx, K. 2011. *Economic and Philosophical Manuscripts of 1844*, Blacksburg, VA: Wilder publications.

Marx, K. and Engels, F. 1998. *The Communist Manifesto*, Beijing: Foreign Languages Press.

Marx, K. and Engels, F. 2019. 'Ruling Class and Ruling Ideas'. In J Storey (ed.), *Cultural Theory and Popular Culture: A Reader*, 5th edition, London: Routledge, 54–55.

Middlemiss, L. 2018. *Sustainable Consumption*, London: Routledge.

Miller, MB. 1981. *The Bon Marche: Bourgeois Culture and the Department Store, 1869-1920*. Princeton, NJ: Princeton University Press.

Moore, JW. 2016a. 'Introduction'. In JW Moore (ed.), *Anthropocene or Capitalocene?* Oakland, CA: Kairos, 1–11.

Moore, JW. 2016b. 'The Rise of Cheap Nature'. In JW Moore (ed.), *Anthropocene or Capitalocene?* Oakland, CA: Kairos, 78–115.

More, T. 2002. *Utopia*, Cambridge: Cambridge University Press.

Ollman, B. 1976. *Alienation: Marx's Conception of Man in Capitalist Society*, Cambridge: Cambridge University Press.

Perkin, H. 1968. *The Origins of Modern English Society*, London: Routledge & Kegan Paul.

Plumb, JH. 1982. 'Commercialization and Society'. In N McKendrick, J Brewer and JH Plumb (eds.), *The Birth of a Consumer Society*, London: Europa Publications, 265–334.

Portman-Stacer, L. 2012. 'Anti-Consumption as Tactical Resistance: Anarchists, Subculture, and Activist Strategy', *Journal of Consumer Culture*, 12:1, 87–105.

Purdy, J. 2015. *After Nature*, Cambridge, MA: Harvard University Press.

Reckwitz, A. 2002. 'Toward a Theory of Social Practice', *European Journal of Social Theory*, 5:2, 243–263.

Ruppert, P. 1986. *Reader in a Strange Land*, Athens, GA: University of Georgia Press.

Sahlins, M. 1976. *Culture and Practical Reason*, Chicago, IL: University of Chicago Press.

Salvage Collective. 2021. *The Tragedy of the Worker*, London: Verso.

Sassatelli, R. 2007. *Consumer Culture: History, Theory and Politics*, London: Sage.

Shelley, PB. 2009. 'A Defence of Poetry'. In *Percy Bysshe Shelley: The Major Works*, Oxford: Oxford World's Classic, 674–701.

Shields, R. 1992. 'The Individual, Consumption Cultures and the Fate of Community'. In R Shields (ed.), *Lifestyle Shopping: The Subject of Consumption*, London: Routledge, 99–113.

Shove, E. 2003. *Comfort, Cleanliness and Convenience*, Oxford: Berg.

Shove, E., Pantzar, M. and Watson, M. 2012. *The Dynamics of Social Practice*, London: Sage.

Shorter, E. 1977. *The Making of the Modern Family*, London: Collins.

Simmel, G. 1957. 'Fashion', *American Journal of Sociology*, 62:6, 541–658.1.

Simmel, G. 1964. 'The Metropolis and Mental Life'. In KH Wolff (ed.), *The Sociology of Georg Simmel*, New York: The Free Press, 409–424.

Stone, L. 1977. *The Family, Sex and Marriage in England, 1500-1800*, Harmondsworth: Penguin.

Storey, J. 2003. *Inventing Popular Culture*, Malden, MA: Blackwell.

Storey, J. 2010. *Culture and Power in Cultural Studies*, Edinburgh: Edinburgh University Press.

Storey, J. 2013. *From Popular Culture to Everyday Life*, London: Routledge.

Storey, J. 2019. *Radical Utopianism: On Refusing to Be Realistic*, London: Routledge.

Storey, J. 2021a. *Cultural Theory and Popular Culture*, 9th edition, London: Routledge.

Storey, J. 2021b. *Consuming Utopia*, London: Routledge.

Storey, J. and McDonald, K. 2013. 'Love's Best Habit: The Uses of Media in Romantic Relationships', *International Journal of Cultural Studies*, 17:2, 113–125.

Trentmann, F. 2017. *Empire of Things*, London: Penguin.

Veblen, T. 1994. *The Theory of the Leisure Class*, Harmondsworth: Penguin.

Vickery, A. 1993. 'Women and the World of Goods: A Lancashire Consumer and Her Possessions, 1751–81'. In J Brewer and R Porter (eds.), *Consumption and the World of Goods*, London: Routledge, 274–301.

Volosinov, VN. 1973. *Marxism and the Philosophy of Language*, London: Seminar Press.

Warde, A. 2017. *Consumption*, London: Palgrave Macmillan.

Watson, M. 2019. 'Sustainable Consumption and Changing Practices'. In M Keller et al. (eds.), *Routledge Handbook on Consumption*, London: Routledge, 343–352.

Weber, M. 1965. *The Sociology of Religion*, London: Methuen.

Williams, R. 1965. *The Long Revolution*, Harmondsworth: Penguin.

Williams, R. 1977. *Marxism and Literature*, London: Verso.

Williams, R. 1980. *Problems in Materialism and Culture*, London: Verso.

Williams, R. 1981. *Culture*, London: Fontana.

Williams, R. 1983. *Keywords*, London: Fontana.

Williams, R. 1989. *Resources of Hope*, London: Verso.

Williams, R. 2010. *Tenses of the Imagination*, Bern: Peter Lang.

Williams, RH. 1982. *Dream Worlds: Mass Consumption in Late Nineteenth Century France*, Berkeley, CA: University of California Press.

Willis, I. 2018. *Reception*, London: Routledge.

Willis, P. 1977. *Learning to Labour: How Working-Class Kids Get Working Class Jobs*, Farnborough: Saxon House.

Wordsworth, W. 2008. *Major Works*, Oxford: Oxford University Press.

Yu, L. 2019. 'China – The Emerging Consumer Power'. In M Keller et al. (eds.), *Routledge Handbook on Consumption*, London: Routledge, 135–145.

Zizek, S. 2019. 'From Reality to the Real'. In J Storey (ed.), *Cultural Theory and Popular Culture: A Reader*, 5th edition, London: Routledge, 433–447.

INDEX

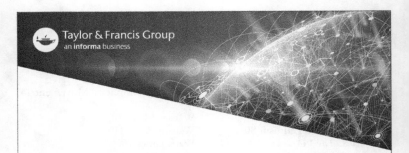